Leaving TRaCKS in THE Snow

A LEGACY OF ENDURING LOVE

STELLA McDOWELL

Printed in the United States of America
ISBN: 978-0-9987430-0-4 (softcover)
ISBN: 978-0-9987430-1-1 (ebook)

Library of Congress Control Number: 2017903482
CouleeSceneBooks, Tempe, ARIZONA

Available from Amazon.com and other retail outlets.

Names of individuals living at the time of publication are used with permission. Some names have been changed when deemed appropriate. Interior photography by Elsie McDowell, Jim McDowell, Joy Peabody, and Pam Clark, used by permission. Photographers unknown for images over 60 years old.

Cover photography by Angela Byram and Joy Peabody, used by permission.

Cover design by Grace Bridges.

Unless otherwise stated, Scripture is taken from the King James Version [KJV].

Dedicated to my parents
Fritz and Mae McDowell
and to my siblings,
Mary Ann, Janice, Jim, and Tim
and to the Lord Jesus Christ,
Who is worthy of our praise and trust
even while the next steps in our lives
are unknown to us.
Without the Lord in our lives
we would not have this
story to share.

Stella McDowell

We will be known forever
by the tracks we leave.
Indian Proverb

Only one life will soon be past;
only what's done for Christ will last.
C. T. Studd
This was on a plaque on the wall of our home
for as long as I can remember.

contents

INTRODUCTION

The dust-to-dust quote echoed silently in our minds. Louder comments from those who stood beside us hinted at the value of this life that was lived out between those two phases of dust. Sentiments like "When I get old, I want to be like your dad" and, "I hope our marriage will be like Fritz and Mae's" summed up the buzzwords of the day.

One speaker's response to those comments was: "If you want to be like Fritz and Mae in your later life, don't wait. It won't just happen. Set your course now." The question is: "How?"

The foundation—what a person believes and the resulting values— gives direction to the decisions a person makes, and the results of those decisions are demonstrated in a person's actions, attitudes, relationships, and emotions. Dad chose God's Word as the foundation for his life.

Just as no two snowflakes are alike, neither are two life stories alike. *Leaving Tracks in the Snow* is not meant to make the reader "be the same" as Fritz or Mae, but to reveal that God can grow a believer in such a way that comments like those expressed at his celebration of life service can

1

also be said for others. Each person's story can reflect something special about what God can do within that person's unique personality and circumstances when he or she seeks to trust and obey the Lord Jesus.

Leaving Tracks in the Snow pulls back the curtain and reveals some of the ways the Master Potter fashioned that pliable dust into the man whose life prompted such comments. An ordinary dust-to-dust life, yes, but an extraordinary life fleshed out within that dust continues to challenge and encourage us to follow the One he sought to follow.

We who knew Dad could borrow Job's words for the telling of his story: "He [God] knows the way I take. When he has tried me, I shall come forth as gold" (Job 23:10).

If Dad were writing this he would more closely identify with David the psalmist. "When I consider thy heavens, the work of thy fingers, the moon and the stars, which thou hast ordained: What is man, that thou art mindful of him?" (Psalms 8:3-4a).

Dad lived and left behind for us a legacy of faith and life lessons. He often asked why he was so blessed. It is we who knew and loved Dad (Fritz to so many) who are the ones who feel blessed because an ordinary man, who loved and lived for the Lord Jesus Christ, touched our lives.

CHAPTER 1

THE FIRE

The horses raced into the familiar lane covered in sweat. Never had Charlie's team been driven so hard. He was delivering mail on the ridge of his rural route in western Wisconsin when a messenger racing toward him flagged him down while yelling, "Charlie! There's a fire in De Soto! Your house is burning!" Even the horses seemed to sense the urgency to get home. They ran past their usual stops, down the winding road to the valley, onward along the picturesque Great River Road that hugs the mighty Mississippi, and up the hill to home.

By the time Charlie pulled on the reins and brought the horses to a halt, he saw little more than blackened embers still smoldering where his home had stood just a few hours earlier. Neighbors were doing their best to console his crying children.

"Maude! Where's Maude?"

Charlie rushed to his wife who had been taken to the McDowells' nearest neighbors. Since the new doctor in town had already arrived, Charlie told him to go ahead and finish treating the burns on Maude's hands and arms. For his wife's face, however, Charlie said they would wait for the older more familiar doctor. There was an element of trust and history with the old doc that had not yet been established with the new one.

Bits of conversation among those who had been first on the scene were gradually sorted out, forming a picture of the sequence of events that had transpired on that indelible day, March 4, 1926.

It was a school day so only the two youngest children were home with their mother. The McDowell family had just purchased a new cook-stove, the kind with an open grate. While his mother was busy in another part of the house, three-year-old Maurice rolled up a piece of paper and made it small enough to partially stuff into a hole of the grate. The tip of the paper ignited instantly and the growing flame scared Maurice. He threw the burning paper into the woodshed just outside the back door. When Maude stepped back into the kitchen, Maurice warned, "Don't go out there!" (A sure sign to any mother that she had better get out there fast!)

In the woodshed Maude saw the burning paper on the floor. Above it was the barrel of kerosene used for fueling the lamps. Beneath the barrel was a small can to catch any drips that might leak from the barrel. In that moment of panic, she reached to move the can out of harm's way but it tipped over and a sudden flash of intense heat and flames leaped at her.

Even in the shock of that frightening moment Maude was cognizant of one thing—the children! They were always the first thought on this mother's mind. She had to get Maurice and one-year-old Beulah outside into the cold March air. Once they were safely out of the house, she collapsed into the snow. Rolling in the white drifts, she cooled her burns and extinguished any flames that had licked at her clothing. She turned back to the burning house with every intention of retrieving important papers from the bedroom, but she could not move. Alerted by the flames and smell of fire, neighbors came on the run and held her back.

Mr. Owens, one of the neighbors, rushed into the house to do what Maude was unable to do. He reappeared with an armload of books with important papers sandwiched in between. Other neighbors tried to pull a few more items from the front rooms before the smoke and the spreading fire engulfed that part of the house. The house would not and could not be saved, but thankfully no lives were lost.

While one neighbor rushed to the business side of the De Soto village to fetch the doctor for Maude's burns another neighbor, Joe McAuley, went about a mile away to get Etta, Jessie, Jenny, Alberta, Fritz, and Alida, the six older children, from school. Details of the day's events were still being retraced in the minds of each of them when daylight yielded to the arrival of the evening's darkness.

The Josephs hustled Charlie and all eight of the children into their home for that first night while the doctors were still giving Mrs. Joseph details regarding Maude's burns and instructions for her care. The doctors had already treated her burns and wrapped her hands, arms, and face with dressings.

That night the losses of the day began to dawn on the family in a practical way. Essentially all of the clothing except what was on their backs was gone. The well-stocked shelves and cellar full of canned goods was no more. Still they were blessed. They had all of their family and they had good neighbors. In the morning some of those neighbors came with a child's wagon filled with basic necessities for the family. Others came with offers to take in some of the children until Charlie could figure out what his next steps would be.

The whole family began to deal with challenges even beyond that of losing their house and being separated within the community. For the children, their mother's face was hidden from them behind her bandages. Her hands were covered with dressings at a time when her loving touch would have been so comforting. Her voice was soft and calming for the sake of the children. Yet she was dealing with her own pain as privately as she could.

Charlie owned a small four-room house and the land across the lane from where their house had stood. The renters there had been planning to move to Cooley Valley, but they graciously relocated earlier than planned, giving the McDowell family a place to stay and be together.

Sixteen-year-old Etta, the oldest of the eight McDowell children, carried many extra responsibilities in helping the family. In the evenings she would hand wash or scrub the family's dirty clothes and hang them up to dry overnight so the very same clothes could be worn the next day. She also took upon herself the role of mothering her siblings as best she could.

Etta missed more school days, but for the other five school-aged children, the upheaval the fire caused was no excuse for them to miss. Charlie insisted that they keep up with their studies and, as much as possible, with their attendance. Perhaps this was his way of trying to maintain some semblance of normalcy in their lives.

A couple known to the children as Aunt Ella Morley and Uncle Dick, a stone mason, arrived to help with the rebuilding. That meant two more adults would be temporarily sharing the small house with the family. As a result some of the children stayed with various neighbors as they had done while waiting for the renters to move. Years later, Etta recalled with tears in her eyes how difficult it was to have the family separated during this trying period. Her motherly instinct, so firmly established during those days after the fire, never left her.

Despite the somber circumstances, wallowing in self-pity would have just been a waste of time. There was work to be done. Charlie had no trouble finding projects for the children to help with whenever school was not in session. Together they would work, and together the family would see their new home rise from the ashes.

Charlie hitched up his team six days a week for his mail route just as he had done before the fire. Left behind each day was old Bob, the gentle horse that even the young children could handle. Bob stood patiently waiting while the children shoveled and scraped dirt and debris into the scoop to clear the site where the fire had turned their house into charred rubble. Then the old horse would respond to their coaxing, pull the scoop up a steep slope, and drag it to the dumping area. That slope would become the location of the new basement steps.

During the fire, exploding canning jars sent shards of glass flying in every direction. Years later Fritz, who was ten years old at the time of the fire, recalled having to be so careful of the sharp pieces of glass mixed in with whatever else had burned. Sometimes in the midst of digging through the debris that had fallen into the old basement, one of the children would find a coin, now blackened, that had been kept in a jar on a kitchen shelf.

Charlie and Maude often repeated and lived by two strong convictions throughout the years: "If you are going to do a job, do it right," and "Whatsoever thy hand findeth to do, do it with thy might" (Ecclesiastes 9:10a). The kids probably heard these sayings often as they cleaned out debris or pounded nails. They were not easily excused from work.

In recalling those days of rebuilding after the fire, Jessie told of an incident about how she missed the nail and hit her finger with a hammer. She requested that her father excuse her from her assignment. Charlie

7

was not so direct as to deny his daughter's request outright, but knowing she was right-handed he wisely responded, "If it's not a finger on your right hand, you can keep working."

The days after the fire were times of learning to put personal preferences aside in order to more quickly have a home where the whole family could once again be together. They helped each other learn skills and think through problems that arose during the rebuilding process. Nobody had to tell them life works best when you put your heads together to come up with a good solution. They learned that firsthand.

The younger children did not fully understand their mother's expressed urgency to be able to move into the new house by Thanksgiving even if it was not totally completed. Maude had been on the sidelines throughout much of the rebuilding project while her burns were healing. Her hands healed, but they were forever scarred. When the old doctor finally took the strips of dressings off her face, the old burned skin came off with them. (This is the way the adults recalled the scene from their childhood memories of what occurred.) She had no scars on her face but she had changed. During this whole time she was pregnant with baby number nine. Hugh was born on December 16, 1926.

What a Christmas! With an ax in one hand Charlie led the way across the lane and up the hill with his troop of kids. Some were following him and some were scampering in various directions, but they all were on the lookout for the perfect Christmas tree. No matter how many trees were deemed perfect in the eyes of the children, Charlie would make the final choice. Knowing the limited space available in the completed part of the house, he would have to choose a small one this year.

Christmas morning came but few gifts could be found under the very sparsely decorated tree in front of the new bay window. Yet, they had the gift of having the complete family together under one roof again. The large family had always been close, but after all they had been through that year, their bond had strengthened as each member had a newfound appreciation for one another. The scent of the freshly-cut Christmas tree mingled with that of the new lumber and overpowered any lingering odors of burnt wood. Surely brighter days were ahead! Surely the unity and closeness they felt that Christmas would last forever.

The family eventually grew to thirteen children. Years later Charlie and Maude's grandchildren would learn there had been a fire, but details were not shared until they, as adults, asked questions about it. Even then blame was not a part of the story. It was simply told as family experience they lived through and grew from.

Left to right, back row: Blaine, Hugh, Alberta, Alida, Beulah, Fritz, Ruby, Maurice, Ruth, Elsie, and Etta.

Front row left to right: Jenny, Charlie, Maude, and Jessie.

CHAPTER 2

McDOWELL PRINCIPLES and PRACTICES

By everyone's account, family insiders and casual observers alike, Charlie was the undisputed authority at the helm of his family. Although he was strict, his children saw him as a tender and loving husband to their mother. Having keen insight into right and wrong, he stood firmly for what was right to the best of his understanding. Respected in the community, by popular vote he served as Justice of the Peace. He was a man who said what he meant and meant what he said, both at home and in the public arena. Once he made a decision, he was not one to budge from it. This did not endear him to everybody. Accusations of being hard-headed and stubborn only made him smile and agree with his accusers.

One blustery winter day Charlie took Maude to a chiropractor in a nearby town for a scheduled appointment. Nobody should have been on the county roads that day with the blinding snow and howling winds. When they walked into the office, the doctor scowled, "Old fools aren't dead yet."

"I told you we'd be here and I always keep my word," Charlie replied.

There was another motivation for him to keep his word, however. He had doubted that a chiropractor could help alleviate Maude's pain and Charlie claimed it would just be a waste of money. So the doctor made a deal with him. If Charlie got Maude to all of her appointments and if the treatments did not help, Charlie would not have to pay. In the end the chiropractor won—and so did Maude.

People in his community did not always agree with Charlie, but he was known as a man who offered leadership and practical assistance when he could. As a mail carrier and employee of the federal government, he was paid with government issued checks. One day in the 1930s—shortly after many banks suddenly closed their doors—Charlie had his check that he had not yet cashed. When he stopped at Halverson's, a rural store on his mail route, Charlie saw a distraught look on the storekeeper's face. The storekeeper had bills that were due but his money was tied up in the bank. Charlie queried him, "If I cash my check here, would that help?"

Upon hearing this offer the storekeeper's countenance brightened. "Charlie, that would be like a gold mine to me!" Apparently government checks were as good as cash to the storekeeper's creditors.

For years after that the storekeeper gave Charlie a heads-up whenever he knew the prices were going to be increased. Charlie did not shop often, but when he did he bought large quantities of flour, sugar, dried fruit, oatmeal, macaroni, and peanut butter. As was the case with most rural families during that time, the majority of what they ate came from their garden. However, there was one special treat that did not come from the garden—ice cream.

Every Fourth of July Charlie bought a five-gallon container of ice cream and the family celebrated the holiday by having a picnic. On this special day the whole family, and friends who happened to join them, could eat as much ice cream as they wanted.

Charlie showed his children by example that they could move mountains when they worked together. Alongside the length of the house was a strip of land that was plenty wide for the double grooved path created by the horse and buggy and later on by the Model T car. Along the edge of that dirt driveway was an embankment. Rains gradually washed away the far side of the flat strip of land causing the driveway to gradually narrow.

Charlie owned the hill on the other side of their lane. In a seemingly never-ending process, Charlie and his sons carved out a huge chunk of that hill, one shovel load and one trailer load at a time, and dumped each load of earth over the embankment. Little by little the driveway was widened enough to accommodate even the wide cars of the 1950s and '60s.

De Soto's resident tailor and hobby artist, Clarence Powell, dreamed of having a museum in town where his art could be displayed. Charlie caught his vision and worked with Clarence until the dream became reality. Mr. Powell's art even earned him recognition at the World Trade Fair in Chicago. "Promise me, Charlie," Clarence said on his death bed, "you will keep my art in Wisconsin." Mr. Powell's museum was not left under Charlie's control, just the art pieces.

To keep his promise to his friend, Charlie got the whole family involved in remaking the no longer used barn into a museum. He and his sons cleaned up the barn, laid a new wood floor, and painted the building. The final needed touches included advertisement signs to be erected along Old Highway 35. What colors would catch the eye of motorists whizzing by at thirty-five or forty miles per hour? What size of stencils should be used so tourists could read the information clearly? The daughters assigned to this task contemplated such questions.

If this conversation was typical of the McDowell conversations, each opinion would be prefaced with "Don't you suppose...?" or "What do you think about...?" They generally communicated their ideas in a way that exhibited consideration of and deference to each other's opinions. They functioned as a team, evidenced in the way they showed respect for one another and for each offered suggestion. Their mutual goal was the success of whatever the project or challenge was that they were addressing rather than personal recognition for an individual's contributions of ideas or skills.

The country museum was quite simple and quaint. A note on the door read that visitors should go to the house and knock if they wanted to see the museum. Charlie would unlock the old barn door. Then, with his spotlight in one hand and a long extension cord trailing behind him, he guided the visitors to each diorama, reciting a memorized speech with much inflection in his voice about each of the Biblical or historical scenes. He showed how Mr. Powell crafted each of the tiny detailed three-dimensional figures in each scene from recycled scraps of fabric, pieces of tin cans, and twigs and grasses, using only simple tools like his jackknife.

As Charlie introduced visitors to various antiques he had collected, he asked, "Do you know what this is?" Or, "Can you guess what this was used for?" His eyes brightened when a visitor nostalgically recalled memories of specific items, or whenever he could stump them with an object. He then carried on the conversation by answering their questions about the use or function of some odd looking antique gadget. Before they left, Charlie invited the visitors to sign their names in a guest book, record where they were from, and leave any comments. If Charlie wasn't home, his daughter Jessie could lead the visitors on this guided tour with the same memorized speech and the same inflections in her voice. She didn't, however, have the same twinkle in her eyes that Charlie had when introducing the museum's antiques.

When the second generation of McDowells could no longer maintain the museum at De Soto, the art pieces were given to an art museum in Sheboygan, Wisconsin, where they could be appreciated and preserved.

As the head of his household Charlie laid down the law and expected full compliance from his children. As the children grew older, he generally did not intervene in a way that would mitigate or soften lessons to be learned due to natural consequences of their actions, especially if they had been properly forewarned. Instead, Charlie's typical response was, "Well, I guess he (or she) will learn his (or her) lesson now." Maude's approach to discipline was usually much milder than that of her husband. If the children got into a disagreement or argument, her comment was, "If you're going to quarrel about it, put it away."

Fritz learned the consequences of making a poor decision the hard way one day near the end of his senior year of high school. Riding on the back of a truck was a normal means of transportation in those days. However, Fritz quickly learned that sitting on a round milk can in the bed of a truck that was going up a steep hill was not a very smart thing to do, especially with other teens also riding in the truck bed. Feeling a bit of a sway Fritz assumed one of the other fellows was trying to tip the can he was sitting on as a way of getting a reaction out of him so he didn't steady himself. As it turned out, none of his companions was up to any trickery. For some reason the truck must have made a sudden jerk, causing the can to tip over and Fritz—along with the milk can—toppled and fell off the back of the truck and onto the road. The can continued to roll downhill, but Fritz landed hard on the pavement. Sharp edges of broken front teeth cut his lips and tongue causing blood to drip from his mouth. The bleeding stopped but he would have to live with broken teeth until he could get dentures. That would take some time so he intentionally kept his mouth shut for his high school graduation picture.

As a rural mail carrier Charlie was on the road six days a week. Since Sunday was his only day to be home, he bypassed the opportunity to take his family to church. Generally, Maude and the girls would attend the Methodist church in town while Charlie stayed home with his sons and together they would do the men's work that needed to be done around the house.

Although the rules of the house incorporated biblical standards of right and wrong, talking about God, faith, and the Bible was done only on Sundays at church—that is, until Maude's father, Grandpa Groves, moved in with the family in 1932. Charlie had grown up knowing Grandpa Groves as his uncle and since his youth Charlie had been taught to respect his elders. Therefore, Grandpa Groves' presence and preferences were generally accepted in the McDowell household. He often requested his daughter to play hymns on the piano during evenings and sometimes the family sang together. In this way biblical truth as expressed through hymns was present in the home.

Grandpa Groves was a gentle man who endeared himself to each one of his thirteen McDowell grandchildren. After his visits with relatives who tapped their maple trees and made their own syrup, he brought maple sugar candy treats home for the family. He made swings for his grandchildren and took time to interact with each one. Grandpa Groves thought the two youngest (identical twin girls) should have look-alike clothes so he provided them with new matching outfits. However, while he was living with them, card games were taboo for children as Grandpa Groves frowned on card playing and his grandchildren honored his convictions.

After ten years of living with and observing the family, Grandpa Groves sensed there was a matter he needed to address. Being a man of gentle wisdom, he would one day take his oldest grandson aside and make a small suggestion; but the thought he would plant in Fritz's mind would lie dormant until just the right time when, in God's perfect plan, that small suggestion would change the course of history for the entire McDowell family.

CHAPTER 3

Taking a Stand

A new customer showed up in Ted Sallander's store in De Soto while Fritz, Ted's twenty-one- year-old clerk, was assisting shoppers. Fritz had been expecting to see her. News of visitors to town traveled fast but Fritz would have known anyway because Ted had mentioned that his sixteen-year-old niece, Mae, from Amery, Wisconsin, was coming for a visit during the summer.

This little village was like a whole new world for this young farm girl. Going into Amery from her farm was an infrequent event for Mae, but here, staying with her aunt and uncle, she was actually living right in the middle of the business section of the village. How fun to just walk over to Uncle Ted's store anytime she wanted to.

The store was not nearly as interesting, however, as the young clerk behind the counter. He was tall, thin, had black hair and clear eyes that to Mae seemed to sparkle when he greeted each customer. She clearly had noticed him and peppered her uncle with what she thought were casual questions about Fritz. Mae began to frequent the store for any excuse she could dream up. Fritz's version of this story was that she would come in and ask for "a penny's worth of candy and mix it up, please."

When Ted asked Mae what she would like to do for fun during her visit, without hesitation she sheepishly suggested, "A date with that clerk in your store would be nice."

Charlie was instrumental in getting a movie show for the community to view which was a big event for the village and even the county. Ted willingly gave his clerk time off work along with a not-so-subtle hint about taking Mae to the show. After the movie Fritz extended the evening by taking Mae for a car ride to Lansing to see the new toll bridge. Before they reached the toll booth, Fritz made a U-turn on the bridge and they headed right back to De Soto. He had been taught well to not buy what you do not need and one could certainly see the bridge without having to cross all the way over to the Lansing side just to pay the toll and turn around. Turning around midway was simply the practical thing to do. Had Mae been making the decision, she would have done the same thing because she was just as practical.

Fritz and Mae became good friends during her visit. But summer would soon be over and Mae wanted to give Fritz something tangible to help him remember her. It had to be something special, something she considered as having great value, something he would save. Before she left for Amery, Mae wrapped her gift for Fritz...a Bible.

After Mae left, a few letters passed between Amery and De Soto. With time they became less frequent. The last one she sent was a "Dear John" type letter.

Charlie and Maude were relieved. They had a very close-knit family and they didn't want anything that might interfere. Fritz's older sisters had some suitors in the past, but the possibility of his daughters marrying and leaving home did not meet with Charlie's approval so each suitor eventually lost his pursuing interest.

Grandpa Groves quietly observed this. By 1942 his grandchildren, some already in their early thirties, seemed to have only bleak hopes of ever having a family of their own. The time had come to have a talk with now twenty-five-year old Fritz. Being a man of gentle wisdom, he made just a little suggestion to this oldest grandson. "Fritz, whatever happened to the girl who gave you that Bible? Why don't you try writing her and find out?" Fritz wasn't sure. Mae had written him that Dear John letter when she felt their long-distance romance wasn't offering much of a future. She had wanted dates like the other girls. Surely by this time she would be married.

This much-loved Grandpa Groves died in October of 1942, but the thought he planted in the mind of his grandson did not die with him.

Fritz pondered his grandfather's suggestion for several months. It had been five years since he had received that fateful letter from Mae. Her birthday would be coming in June. He wondered…surely by this time she would be married…but maybe not…but she probably is…but maybe not…. Finally Fritz quietly and carefully chose an appropriate birthday card and dropped it in the mail with the simple note: "If you are married, just throw this away. If you are not, could we start writing?"

Mae was not married. But she was engaged and working in Minneapolis by the time Fritz mailed the card. For her birthday she decided to board a bus and surprise her fiancé in Amery. When she showed up unannounced at his house, he was surprised all right! But he was definitely not delighted. He was happily entertaining another girl in his house at that very moment! Mae removed his ring from her left hand. It was clearly over between them. He would drive her to her family farm home. His new girl hopped into the car beside him while Mae climbed in last. She was pinned between the passenger side car door on her right, with his new girlfriend pressing in on her left side.

Only the lump in her throat and the pressing of her lips together tightly kept Mae silent. If she spoke even a word on that ride home, she knew the floodgate of tears would give way and the wounds of her heart would surface and humiliate her even more. Finally, the car turned onto the dirt road to her farm. Barely had it stopped in front of the house before Mae tugged on the door handle and jumped out. She must get into the shelter of her home before the dammed-up emotions broke through.

Mae's mom was not surprised. She knew this time would come. Better now than after a wedding, she must have been thinking. There had been reports of Mae's fiancé dating other girls while Mae was away working in Minneapolis. Both friends and family had warned her, but Mae had refused to believe them. Now the truth could no longer be denied.

Mae's mom wrapped her arms around her daughter and wiped Mae's tears with her always available apron hankie. She held her daughter until the sobs softened and Mae was able to talk. Devastated! Humiliated! Rejected! Surely unlovable! "Some birthday!" She paused to catch her breath. "How could he do this?" Though she couldn't put voice to all her emotions, her mother knew the meaning of the words she could not fully express. Life had never seemed so dark and hopeless.

"Maybe this will help." Her mother pulled an envelope off the shelf. "This just arrived for you." It was June 1943. While life was seemingly at its very worst to Mae, God was up to doing something amazingly good.

If Mae had received that card a month earlier, or even a week earlier, she would have tossed it. Instead she now wrote back. "No, I'm not married."

Mae resumed her job in Minneapolis with a lot of "what next" questions on her mind. In July she met some girls attending Trinity Bible College in Chicago. That seemed like a good next option so she enrolled for the fall semester. Meanwhile, Fritz rushed a letter to Mae's Minneapolis address. After a couple letters passed between them, he planned a train trip to see her.

Fritz met Mae at her sister's house where she had been staying, and they went for a walk to the nearby park. By the time the two of them returned later that day, observers knew that Fritz and Mae would be a couple.

In September Mae stopped in De Soto while en route to college. Fritz also made a few trips to see her in Chicago. Before Thanksgiving Mae visited La Crosse for the funeral of a cousin who had died in the war. Fritz borrowed a car and drove the thirty-mile river road from De Soto to La Crosse to spend some time with her. He treated her to lunch at the Bodega cafeteria. From there they drove to the Riverside Park. That afternoon they had an eternity changing conversation.

Mae had learned things at the college that she so much wanted to share with Fritz. But how was she to condense so much into a little conversation? She didn't feel capable of explaining something so important. "Lord, help me," she silently prayed. Then she jumped into the subject without thinking he could be offended by anything that was true. "Well," she started, "all of us are born with sin—even the very good people, good people like you." If Fritz was offended, he did not show it. He loved this girl. He wanted to know all about her and if this was important to her, he would listen. She explained that Jesus Christ came not just to be a Christmas baby but to live a perfect life, and then, willingly pay the price for our sin.

She read Romans 3:23: "For the wages of sin is death; but the gift of God is eternal life through Jesus Christ our Lord." Then she explained, "The wages or what we earn by our sin, is death, but Jesus took that penalty, that wage, of death for us so He could give us a gift—eternal life…heaven."

"I thought heaven was for people who live good lives. I guess I never really thought much about why Jesus died," Fritz said.

"Good works can never earn us a right standing before God," Mae told Fritz, quoting Titus 3:5: "Not by works of righteousness which we have done but according to his mercy he saved us, by the washing of regeneration, and renewing of the Holy Ghost." She continued, "Sin separates us from God, but Jesus' death, His burial, and His resurrection broke the barrier that separated us. He's the bridge between man and God. Because of Jesus, we can have a relationship with a holy God."

"Why do we always hear about how we should be doing good then?"

"I'm not saying we should not be good. Living a good life is great, but that does not change the fact that all the good things people do still cannot measure up to God's requirement of righteousness. Good works should be the result of our love for Jesus for all He has done for us. You know, when you love someone you want to please that person."

Fritz, having fallen in love with Mae, already knew that, but he still had a question. "So Mae, you think Jesus is the way for a person to go to heaven?"

"It's not what I think, it's what the Bible says," Mae replied. Turning to John 3:16-17, she read, "God so loved the world, that he gave his only begotten Son, that whosoever believeth in him should not perish, but have everlasting life. For God sent not his Son into the world to condemn the world; but that the world through him might be saved." She looked up from her Bible. "God gave His Son in order to give us salvation but, of course, that gift, like any gift, is not ours until we accept it."

Fritz quietly considered all that Mae had shared before speaking. "I've never fit the pieces together like this before." When he understood that God loved him so much that He sent His Son to die for his sin, tears ran down his cheeks. Fritz right then admitted to God what God already knew—that he was a sinner—and Fritz accepted this gift of salvation. It was November 1943.

On Mae's next trip from Chicago to De Soto, the now twenty-seven-year old Fritz had a ring for her. They set their wedding date for April 1944. Mae returned to finish her semester at college and to work at her laundry job near the college until mid-April. Could any bride be happier? God had protected her from marrying the wrong man. He had preserved her for this one man, Fritz McDowell. God is so good! Theirs was a mutually shared love and commitment to one another.

Charlie and Maude did not eagerly embrace the idea of one of their children leaving the nest. Some younger siblings saw their oldest brother taking a stand on this matter as paving the path for them to venture out and get married someday too. They would not oppose Fritz getting married. However, a couple of the older sisters were not happy about it as marriage for them earlier, they expressed, had not been an acceptable option so why would it be okay now? Clearly, the harmony within the family had hit a sour note.

This idea of marriage certainly was no rash move of rebellion by an immature teen. Fritz had learned well at his father's side. They had worked side by side: tinkering under a car down in the pit, moving the hill, plowing up the garden, chopping wood, plus, a host of other things. His father had entrusted him with much responsibility of watching over the household while the mail route kept Charlie away. Fritz was meticulous in his math and record keeping skills. His diligence, his attention to detail, and his friendliness had won him a job with the railroad.

Though he was the oldest son and often carried responsibilities for the family, he did not lord it over his siblings. The attitude of each of the McDowell children was that each one had different abilities and each person's skill was a valuable contribution. They were a team working together; they could help each other, learn from each other, and explore each other's ideas for solving problems. For instance, one year the brothers teamed up in the toolshed and made their own roller skates. Another year they got tired of cleaning potatoes from the garden for winter storage so they headed to the toolshed again and came up with a potato scrubbing machine. It worked so well, it not only scrubbed the dirt off the potatoes but the skins as well. It was considered a failure but they learned from the process and disassembled it to use parts for another invention. They bounced ideas back and forth and set out to create new ways of improvising whatever their latest project was.

Fritz was a peace-loving man. How could getting married pose such a threat to family unity? He loved his parents and siblings and cared deeply for them and their feelings, but he also wanted to have his own family and carry on that same kind of love and closeness for a next generation. He was learning that God had a plan and purpose for his life and that Mae and marriage would be a major part of that plan. Fritz was committed to the belief that he and Mae should live their lives together as Mr. and Mrs., for better or for worse, for the rest of their lives.

Maude's heart ached as the car carrying Fritz and Reo—a family friend who would be the best man—pulled out from their driveway. By this time, she and Charlie had reluctantly agreed to the marriage. Years later Maude would write a letter to Mae expressing they had not been opposed to Mae, but they knew if one married, the rest of their children would soon follow. They feared that they would no longer be the close family unit the fifteen of them had become.

Fritz laid on the backseat, wincing with sciatica pain. Why this? Why now did he have to suffer with an episode of such pain? Reo did his best to maneuver between bumps on the 170-mile road trip to Amery. Regardless of the challenges, Fritz was on his way to get his bride.

CHAPTER 4

AND SO IT BEGAN

And so it began at the little country Apple River Church. Mae had left Chicago and her college friends in mid-April of 1944 and was welcomed home to make quick preparations for the simple wedding. Reo pulled off Highway Eight onto the dirt lane that circled to the front of the farmhouse. The windmill whirled with the early spring breeze while under its shadow only a wisp of new life barely peeked through the almost barren flower garden. Soon there would be a miniature forest of flowers springing up, adding a fragrant loveliness when the breezes were not downwind of the barn.

If Mae had any illusions of her knight in shining armor arriving to sweep his bride off her feet up and into his arms, that dream would have been shattered. Life is not really like that. Instead Fritz's sciatic pain made every move an effort. He could hardly walk. In planning for their marriage, their commitment already had been made for better, for worse, in sickness and in health. They would be together until death would part them.

It was not a laughing matter to be in so much pain on his wedding day, but years later Fritz would teasingly say, "Mae caught me because I couldn't run."

The plan was that Reo would be the best man and Fritz's brother Maurice would be his groomsman. Fritz's siblings, Maurice and Beulah, had gone to Rice Lake which was not far from Amery. They were visiting Beulah's college friend who just happened to be the brown-eyed beauty who captured Maurice's heart. If Fritz could pave the way for one of the McDowell kids to marry, Maurice would prepare to take the plunge too.

Planning the wedding had been simple. The vows were the standard ones of the day, which would be read by the pastor from his little black book. Fritz and Mae repeated those words, knowing they were making serious vows before God and their guests. Though Ila Mae Hansen sang the popular wedding music of the day, the messages of "Because" and "I Love You Truly" were the real expressions of the hearts of this bride and groom. Mae's sisters, Fern and Helen, stood to the left of Mae. Mae's flower girl nieces, Elvera and Marilyn, with oversized bows in their hair, impatiently fidgeted in their appointed place. Sometime between the minister's statements, "If anyone knows of any reason this couple should not be married, let him speak now or forever hold his peace," and the "I now pronounce you husband and wife," some people within earshot of six-year-old Marilyn broke into muffled giggles. She interrupted the solemn service announcing her personal crisis, "Aunt Mae, my bow fell out!"

The wedding party and guests went back to the farmhouse for the reception and watched the bride and groom open their gifts. Some were the common gifts of the day like pillowcases, towels, a cookbook, a food grinder, a rolling pin, and bowls. Unusual gifts included a bottle of vanilla, a one-half gallon of syrup, and a quilt top. The common cash gifts were in the amounts of one or two dollars, but there was one twenty-dollar gift. Every gift was received with gratitude. Mae recorded each gift on the card and preserved those cards in a brown scrapbook that she kept for even her great-grandchildren to see.

The newlyweds spent their first two nights of married life at the farm with Mae's family. Younger sister Fern had prepared a treat for them. She patiently waited on the opposite side of their bedroom door until either the navy beans she had hidden in the sheets were discovered, or she could no longer hide her giggles.

By the third day of their marriage the new couple was already discovering that the best of plans can be changed, especially when the need of someone else calls for attention. They boarded the bus for Minneapolis with the excitement of starting their new life together. Mae's older sister Lucile was hosting a bridal shower for Mae there, and Mae was looking forward to introducing her husband to friends she had worked with a year earlier. As they arrived at Lucile's, so did a message from the family in De Soto. Fritz's mother had suffered what was thought to be a heart attack.

The newlyweds caught the next train for Wisconsin. The shower went on as scheduled, but Mae would not be attending her own bridal shower. Instead of a day of joyful reunion with friends, she rode the train with her groom. Every click of the rails carried them closer to the bedside of her new mother-in-law, and the likelihood of a cool reception. They had no way of knowing what Maude's health status would be by the time they arrived. Mae feared that perhaps there would be insinuations from the family that she was the cause of their mother's health crisis.

Once Maude recovered, Charlie planned an ice cream social in honor of the newlyweds. Mae really wanted a corsage for the occasion,

31

but Fritz refused, saying, "Mae, we can't buy one. My family would consider that an unnecessary expense." He wanted so much to honor his family's values as much as he could and not give any of them an excuse for any more negative attitudes.

Fritz's sixteen-year-old sister Elsie was gifted, even in her teen years, to be sensitive to the feelings of others and take action to make others feel special and loved. Wearing a corsage for special events was a common practice of the day. Mae did not express her desire for one to anyone other than her husband. Yet, Elsie, aware of that common custom, enlisted her twenty-year-old sister, Beulah, to help and together they created a corsage for Mae. This was a kind act of love and acceptance which Mae treasured at a time when she so needed it.

To surrender your own desires for the good of others, especially for his family, had been a part of who Fritz had become. It would take time for him to learn how to sort out his new roles. Mae too had come into marriage with her own ideas and desires for what their marriage would be. All couples have to figure this out together, and that Fritz and Mae would do. What was beyond them, though, was the ability for both of them to feel the unity and the sense of belonging which had so characterized the McDowell family before. How could God work out this problem? They were just an ordinary young couple faced with a challenge too big for them. Could God really do for their situation above and beyond their expectations? While they waited, they continued adjusting to married life with all its blessings and challenges…and they made thirty-mile weekend trips to De Soto.

CHAPTER 5

MAKING ADJUSTMENTS

There was a flurry of activity in La Crosse in 1944. With WWII in full swing, soldiers in training, or waiting on orders, packed the barracks at Camp McCoy. The government gave Fritz a F4 status which meant he had failed the physical so he would not be going to war.

Still he would have a role in the war efforts. Soldiers and military equipment crisscrossed the country by train. Fritz worked for the railroad doing his part in getting soldiers and supplies to their proper destinations.

The Camp McCoy military families caused an overflow of population into nearby La Crosse, making available housing scarce. Finally, the newlyweds found a small sparsely furnished upstairs apartment with wide gaps between the floorboards. The springboard of the furnished bed broke so they slept on the floor. That was manageable for the young newlyweds. One night Mae unintentionally trapped a bee in the crack between the floorboards under her which definitely was not a laughing matter at the time. Both Mae and Fritz would tell the story later of Mae and her bee sting with a twinkle in their eyes.

Mae was skilled in the made-from-scratch kind of cooking and baking and took great pleasure in making tasty meals for her groom. Fritz's habit was to persevere in his work and he often had trouble leaving an unfinished task, even to eat. One day his frustrated bride called him for what seemed the umpteenth time, "Oh, Mr. McDowell, dinner is ready!" She had made biscuits, but by the time Fritz actually got to the table they were cold. Always one to tease, he tapped one on his plate while knocking the underside of the table with his knuckle, making it sound like the biscuit was hard and dry. Then he said with a twinkle in his eyes, "It didn't even break the plate." This new husband sent his bride into tears. He had a lot to learn about teasing without hurting the feelings of his young wife, and Mae had to learn to forgive when her feelings were hurt. She didn't forget the event but she did forgive.

One practice Fritz and Mae wisely worked at implementing early in their marriage became advice they would share with other couples later. They would not go to sleep until they resolved issues between them which had come up during the day.

Almost every weekend the couple drove the thirty-mile trip to De Soto to be with the McDowell family. It was not easy, but Fritz felt it was the right thing to do. Mae was a hardworking farm girl so she pitched right in with the gardening, harvesting, canning, and cooking. Filed in her brown scrapbook of wedding cards and list of wedding gifts, she added lists of what she had helped can during those weekend trips. It seems that this was one of the few activities she felt she could participate in and feel included as a part of the family.

Another bonding experience showed up unexpectedly in the blackberry patch. Never had Mae participated in such a huge harvest of berries. Of course, never had she picked berries with such a large crew of pickers who knew the locations of the best blackberry patches. They tramped through the grasses together, moving from one bush to the next as a unit. Together they were pricked by the thorns from the bushes and together they filled pails and pails of berries. When the day ended, someone took a picture of the team of smiling pickers and their harvest. Was there a hint of softening hearts?

Mae was a great cook and everything tasted better when her hands joined the others in the meal preparations. Even Fritz's older sisters appreciated her cooking, and her skilled help with the kitchen work. All that work and all those weekends they spent at De Soto did not, however, give her the sense of acceptance she had hoped for in the hearts of two of the older sisters. But God was in the process of creating an answer! Hints of the miracle God was working out wasn't noticed for a few months. Once realized, hearts began to change.

Fritz and Mae's first baby was born shortly before Thanksgiving 1945. As the McDowells celebrated the birth of the Christ Child that Christmas, they had a whole new understanding of what a blessing and what a difference the reception of a baby can make. It had been a long time since a new baby had joined this family who so loved babies. Likely the reason there were only thirteen children in the family was more related to Maude's biological clock than the thought that thirteen was enough. Each of Charlie and Maude's babies had been wanted and loved. Maude had rocked her babies and directed the older children with their responsibilities from her rocking chair.

Oh, the joy of having a newborn in the De Soto house again, at least on weekends. Oh, to wrap your arms around a swaddled baby and hold it closely! This first baby of the next generation was passed between the waiting arms of all twelve of Fritz's siblings. Forgiveness and mutual love for this baby melted those negative attitudes into nonexistence. This baby was the key God used to unlock the door of hearts resistant to the idea of in-laws coming into the family or, more specifically, of family members leaving the nest. The message of peace on earth, goodwill to men, became a reality for the whole McDowell family the Christmas of the first grandchild.

The McDowells would continue to be a very close-knit family. Considering the bond between Mae, Etta, and Alberta over the rest of their lives, no one would have ever guessed how rocky their relationship had been at the beginning.

That baby brought another big change. Charlie and Maude would from that time on be called Grandpa and Grandma McDowell. Fritz and Mae would be known as Dad and Mom. And that baby? That's where I came into the story. All I knew was that I was loved, safe, and secure—whether in the arms of my parents, my grandparents, or my aunts and my uncles. I was the first of many babies who would be eagerly welcomed into the McDowell family

Gradually the little family did not make the thirty-mile trip to De Soto every single weekend. On the weekends we did not travel, Mom and Dad began establishing their own Sunday patterns. A little Free Church had started in La Crosse not far from their apartment. Mom was anxious to go as it was affiliated with the Bible College she had attended in Chicago, but Dad hesitated. The sciatic pain had resurfaced. Walking was painful and sitting was worse. How could he go to church and sit for a whole hour?

Once the young pastor, John Ellefson, realized Dad's situation, he came up with a solution. "Fritz," he said, "I've got a cot set up behind the last pew by the coat rack. It will be there every Sunday for you if you need to lie down."

That was the beginning of Dad and Mom's friendship with Pastor

John and Rosie Ellefson. The two couples shared experiences as first-time parents as their daughter was about six months older than I was. The couples bonded and their friendship continued throughout their lifetimes.

First steps are always small, but set the pattern for each new step. Both Dad and I were learning to walk. I was graduating from taking a few wobbly steps holding somebody's hand to walking solo while Dad was learning to take steps in his spiritual life. John took Dad under his wing to mentor him as a new believer. Everything about having a relationship with the Lord and about leading his family as a Christian husband and father was new for Dad.

Mom really looked forward to Wednesday night prayer meetings. Their little church united with another church to become Moody Memorial Evangelical Free Church. By this time Dad had moved his family out of the small apartment into a house on Market Street. He would babysit while Mom walked to the prayer meetings. Later Wednesday night meetings became a regular part of life for the whole family.

At the beginning, in a spirit of obligation or duty, Dad would drop a quarter into the offering plate on Sunday mornings. Considering the wages of that day, a quarter was a token gift but not a tithe. As he grew in his understanding of all that God had done for him, he grew in his willingness to give to the Lord.

In time he would give a tithe, and later it would be much more. Though the offering plate was passed each Sunday there was no pressure on the congregants to give.

Before the days when most men had two suits in their closet, George Antello, a missionary from Bolivia, was visiting. George didn't advertise it, but he had no suit. Dad observed that, took his own suit jacket off, and handed it to him. "Try it on, George." It fit so Dad said, "It's yours. You need this more than I do as you go visiting churches in the States." Dad was growing in generosity. He literally gave the shirt (or suit jacket) off his back to meet the need of this missionary.

Hospitality began with a bang, and grew into blessings as well as challenges, as people came into our home in ever increasing numbers.

The house on Market Street had two bedrooms. When Mom and Dad saw a need they met it. Reo, the best man from their wedding, was in need of a place to stay. Not only did they make room for him in their home, but Mom ironed his many, many shirts. She was motivated to help Reo find a loving mate (who also could iron shirts) so she went looking. Reo had known Dad's sister Alida as a friend of the family, but through Mom's matchmaking efforts their relationship blossomed. This couple married and Reo's room was vacant, but just for a short time.

Mom's brother Herb had just finished his service in the Navy and soon found a job in La Crosse. He had no time for the Lord or for church in his life, but Mom and Dad had time and room for Herb in their lives. He moved into the vacated bedroom. Mom came home one evening from church. "Herb, I met a very special young nanny at church tonight. Would you like to meet her?"

She contacted Ona, the nanny, and arranged for both Herb and Ona to attend a church social. That was the beginning of a new life for Herb. Mom and Dad's example and friendship helped another couple find their perfect match. Eventually Herb and Ona became united in their faith in Jesus—and in marriage.

Another guest for a couple nights was a shirttail relative of Dad's who had become a Christian. Eva, a single missionary, was the first personal introduction to missions for our family. Her stories—or maybe just her presence in our home—stirred an interest in missions that would span many years and inspire personal involvement. The pattern was gradually forming that would characterize in a major way how Dad and Mom would live their lives.

CHAPTER 6

A BIRTHDay Present

On the weekends we did go to De Soto, one beep of the horn announcing our arrival brought aunts and uncles racing to the driveway, arms outstretched, hoping to be the first to reach their niece. When it was time to leave, there would be a circle of aunts and uncles as well as Grandma and Grandpa McDowell each in line for a good-bye kiss. If by great effort someone got in line twice, the process of making the rounds had to start over.

Each of my aunts and uncles thought up little things to teach me; silly things, but my responses brought obvious joy especially to the one who had come up with the idea. Uncle Hugh taught me to put one finger in the air and say "Hi." How simple, how silly, but it certainly entertained them. Even as a toddler I caught on quickly how to bring joy to the ones who so lavished love and attention on me. After I learned to stand, Dad would hold me by my feet, raise me up above the heads of our captive audience and balance me. I had no fear. I knew the security of being held safely in Dad's hands, and I knew delight when he swooshed me down into his arms. Children were both the object and the source of pure joy in Grandpa and Grandma's house.

Aunt Etta had a job at a photo shop in La Crosse. The shop's owner was planning an advertisement sign to be posted in the city buses and he needed a pint-sized model. Etta of course knew a perfect model for the picture. "Aw, sure, everybody thinks their baby would be the perfect subject" would have been his likely response. However, Etta was right. I met the approval of the owner and the photographer.

Etta chuckled with delight as she took charge of me for the day. She dressed me in a polka-dotted pink and white sun suit with a matching bonnet. I climbed into decorated oversized hat boxes and peeked over the top for one pose. From experience Etta knew exactly how to play and tease with peekaboo and a host of other creative games that drew out from me the desired expressions with eyes bright and sparkling that the photographer aimed for. So, the poster child highlighted in the photo shop's advertisement on the city buses was a point of pride for the McDowell family.

Grandpa had a rule with his thirteen children which continued on at least for a while with the grandchildren. If you did not finish what was on your plate, it would be saved and presented to you again at the next meal. Even though I was at De Soto often, the food prepared by Grandma or the aunts just didn't taste like food my mom made. Stewed tomatoes or creamed kidney beans on bread could not be enticed to pass beyond my seemingly immature taste buds. I often did not want, or could not, or would not eat what was placed before me.

Anticipating contention between Grandpa and me about the cold food on my plate, my aunts would take me into the kitchen along with my plate of uneaten food. Etta or Jenny would come to my rescue to finish eating whatever was left so I was not made to "endure" that same food for the next meal. Now that's real love! Grandpa had to know what was going on. By pretending ignorance, he did not have to acknowledge defeat to this little granddaughter. (He did soften through the years. The rule for younger cousins was that they had to at least try a bite of whatever was on their plate. After a long time of sitting and staring at the one item on his plate, one of the younger cousins asked, "Grandpa, could you try me on something different?")

On my second birthday I was joyfully entertaining the big family who considered this day as special, though I was oblivious to anything unusual going on. Dad and Mom, especially Mom, were a bit preoccupied with the process of the delivery of a present. Instead of being wrapped in paper with a bow, my gift was wrapped in a pink receiving blanket. Mary Ann joined the family on my birthday.

Three years later Mary Ann and I became big sisters to another baby girl, Janice. By baby number three, Mom and Dad were not too secretively hoping for a boy. The doctor, knowing their desire, announced as Janice was born, "It's a girl and she's the best one yet." Two years later they finally heard the news, "It's a boy!" Dad finally had a son, Jimmy Boy. Not that "Boy" was part of his name, but it was an added emphasis that here, finally, was a son!

Love and attention was not lavished on one child over another. Love did not have to be divided with each addition. Love only multiplied with the arrival of each one.

CHAPTER 7

Home as a Haven

There was only one problem about living in our home on Market Street. That one problem became a giant Mom could not conquer. Even through the difficult times of valleys and dark shadows, God was still the Shepherd leading our family to greener pastures.

Our front door and living room window faced the front door and living room window of our neighbors. Between those two front doors were two adjoining yards. The neighbor children, Julie and Bobby, were the same ages as Mary Ann and me. All four were welcome to play in either of the adjoining yards. Lots of playing and snacks of saltine crackers passed between the two houses. The moms of both houses could see the comings and goings of the children from their windows. That was the good side.

Our house was back to back with the next house on the street. Dad gave us specific instructions to play in the yards where both mothers could see us from their windows. Becky, the girl who had come to live in the house backing up to ours, came sometimes to play in the two adjoining yards, and that often meant trouble.

If Becky fell off her bike or stubbed her toe on a crack in the sidewalk, no matter her childhood calamity, it was always the fault of us kids. Becky often would head for her home crying or with complaints about one of us. That would send her mother, a redheaded fireball, into aggressive action. More than once this mother marched around her house to bang on our front door. Out of fear, and usually not out of guilt, Mary Ann and I learned to run and hide under Mom and Dad's bed if we heard this neighbor at the door.

Her angry accusations would start out with "Your girls..." and she would go on to detail what Becky said we had done. Once we even heard her snap, "If you can't whip your kids, I'll do it for you." Mom informed the neighbor that she and Dad could discipline their own children. After an encounter with her, Mom would often be in tears. Of course we were questioned and if it was justified, we would be disciplined. Mom could differentiate between expressions of guilt or innocent fear on the faces of her girls.

Sometimes just stepping out the backdoor to hang laundry on the clothesline stirred up emotions of fear for Mom. Experience had taught her that she could become the object of angry outbursts if this neighbor was in an agitated mood. (Years later after this neighbor's death Mom and Dad learned that she had not been well, but at the time they were unaware that such actions could possibly be a health-related issue.)

With summer coming Mom's stress was building. Mary Ann and I would soon be out of school for the summer break, and Janice and Jimmy had joined the family by this time which meant four kids playing outside. As protector and provider, Dad knew he had to find a new home for Mom's sake.

It was well-known that Highway 61 on the Minnesota side of the Mississippi River would be under reconstruction and homes in its path would be eliminated. How long until the new road would be constructed? No one knew, but in the meantime, one could find a good deal on a house along the highway which would become a haven for our family. Dad would not delay the move by waiting for a buyer for the house in La Crosse. It would be easier to find a renter for it.

The last day of school came and so did the day of the move. Dad made a left turn off old Highway 61 and announced, "We're almost there." The four kids sat on the edge of their seats with faces pressed to the window for their first look at their new home.

I had just finished third grade, Mary Ann first grade, and Janice was a preschooler anxious to catch up with her big sisters. Jimmy Boy was a bundle of boyish energy and ready for adventure even though he was just a toddler. Mom breathed a sigh of relief to be ten miles away from the old neighborhood. Dad was trusting that this was the right place God had led him to for his family's needs.

One more left turn onto a narrow gravel road and the car stopped. We tumbled out, and four pairs of little legs were on the run. What a huge yard, and a garden the size of about three city lots. Dad turned the key in the lock and opened the door to a new life for the family.

Mary Ann, Janice, and I scrambled from one room to another, each claiming which of the four bedrooms would be our first choice. There were nicks and crannies to discover in the house but so much more to explore outdoors. Jimmy was already on the run and not necessarily in the same direction as the girls. We ran as far as the backyard, and then ran back to the house yelling, "Dad! Mom! They forgot their dog!" A black cocker spaniel was pulling at her chain, barking and eagerly trying hard to reach us…to greet us.

Dad laughed, "No. They couldn't take her to their new house. She's ours." Mary Ann made friends with dogs much faster than I. She and Jimmy especially were thrilled with Patsy. Having a dog and living in the country seemed to go together.

Mom divided her time between unpacking and getting her hands into the dirt to plant her garden. Thoughts raced through her mind. "The rows and rows of mature raspberry bushes in the garden could be ignored this year until the berries ripened then…" and she was already thinking of chores for us.

The first visitors to drop in were not at first recognized as neighbors. Bees! They lived up the gravel road just at the turn, an easy walk or a quick bike ride away. Ben, an old widower, showed up at our door with a metal pail with a tightly sealed cover. "Honey," he said holding out the pail. We had never seen honey with the honeycomb before. "I just wanted to stop in and meet the new neighbors. You might be see'n some of my bees around here. Just want your little ones to know they don't have to be afraid of them." He went on, introducing us to how to live with honeybees. "Don't bother them and they won't bother you. They're our friends." Ben had the appearance of being a gentle old man. His face was tanned and weathered, and his eyes seemed a bit sunken like sometimes happens to very old people. His gait was slow but steady. He would be a good neighbor.

Dad knew that this country home would mean a long daily commute for him for work. What would they do about Sundays? There were two churches in Dresbach...the same kind that were in the town where Dad had grown up. By now Dad and Mom were growing in their faith and in understanding God's Word. Would they continue to drive on Sundays to La Crosse? Or should they make a church in town their choice? Maybe they were to share with others there, like Ben, what they had learned about having a personal relationship with God.

They sought advice from Pastor Carroll Anderson, the new pastor at their church in La Crosse. Pastor Anderson wisely counseled, "Yes, you would be a blessing in your new community by participating in the church there, but your children are your first responsibility. Consider where they, where you, will be likely to continue growing spiritually."

Ease and convenience were not Mom and Dad's priority. Sunday they woke us earlier than usual, and we arrived at our usual time to the church in La Crosse. Mom and Dad chose to make personal sacrifices in order to provide the best opportunity for their children to be taught God's Word. Even with a good church home, they did not leave this responsibility only up to the church, the pastor, or the Sunday school teachers. They followed their fairly regular pattern of Bible story readings appropriate for the attention level of the children or Mom would practice telling whatever lesson she would be teaching in Sunday school or vacation Bible school. Evening prayer was consistently a family affair unless we had been to church for an evening service which would be considered our devotions for the night. When Dad worked evenings, Mom and we kids still prayed together at bedtime. In time, and when we were old enough to read, we began personal devotions instead of the family time together.

Whether we as children remembered meeting the missionaries or not we prayed for them by name on a nightly basis. Two of those missionaries, Eleanor and Willard, came home on furlough from Venezuela. Eleanor had grown up in La Crosse. Though they would travel in the States during most of their furlough, they needed a home base. As was so typical of my parents to meet a need if they could, they invited Eleanor and Willard to consider our home their stateside home. Their mail came to our post office box and whenever they stayed with us, they had the huge enclosed porch as their private quarters—except when Mom needed to get into the big freezer in that room.

The first night these missionaries stayed overnight, they participated in our family devotions. When Jimmy prayed for them by name as we always did, Mom and Dad explained, "This is the Eleanor and Willard we pray for." It seemed to be a revelation that the names we prayed for were real people. Eleanor and Willard often shared the story of Jimmy, the little boy who prayed for them.

During the years in Dresbach, Dad sometimes worked swing shifts. This meant he would often be on rotation requiring him to work the graveyard shift on Saturday night. When on this schedule, he drove the ten miles home, picked up the family and drove back to La Crosse for church. Mom did not drive at this time so it was up to Dad to see that his family got to church. It certainly was not easy. He made personal sacrifices to see that his family would be where he knew we should be. When anyone of us put up a fuss about not wanting to go to church, we were not given the option of staying home. (At least this was the case during the years I lived at home.)

When Dad worked day shifts, we almost always had company for Sunday dinner. Our typical Sunday company menu included beef roast, potatoes and gravy, garden corn, maybe green beans, lots of pickles, and raspberry shortcake—prepared as much as possible before we headed out for our ten-mile trip to church. Sometimes Mom knew who would be coming for Sunday dinner and sometimes she or Dad invited visitors once we got to church. The size of the visiting family or the ages of their kids did not hinder guests from being invited.

Often after working a weeknight shift, Dad stopped for one of the older widows from church to come home for the day "to help Mom." Mostly though, it was to be of help to them in their loneliness. The ironing board was set up in the kitchen when it was Mrs. Peterson's turn to come. That way, she and Mom could talk as they worked. In spite of being old, Mrs. Peterson had unusually dark hair with tight curls and dark-rimmed thick glasses. Mom always made sure she had leftover potatoes to send home for Mrs. Peterson's next batch of her Norwegian lefsa—a potato-based soft flat bread cooked on a griddle much like Mexican tortillas.

Another widow, Sadie, was a fairly short heavyset woman with wiry salt-and-pepper gray hair who always greeted us with tight hugs and happy sounding groans, as if that added emphasis to her loving hugs. Her specialty was mending and sewing. Because her own children had seemingly abandoned her years earlier, it was no secret she considered us like grandchildren to her.

Pastor and Mrs. Anderson had children similar to our ages and were frequent guests. Sometimes when we children ran through the living room, Pastor and Dad would be listening to a ball game on the radio, or years later, when we finally got a black-and-white TV, they would be watching the game. They were just like any good friends with more than one interest to share.

When people with kids came, all of us were excused to play or climb the bluffs behind the house while the women did dishes and talked. We were of the opinion that city kids loved to come and romp through the woods and climb the hills with us. The rule about climbing the bluffs was that we could go anyplace as long as we could still see our house so we would always be able to find our way home.

One place we took only special friends to was what we referred to as our gold mine. This was quite a hike, so often we did not have time to go that far on Sunday afternoons. A ravine between two hills narrowed until deeper into the hills the two sides came together. Trees lined both edges of the steep slopes. As the ravine narrowed, the roots from trees on one side reached over to the other side of the ravine, exposing the roots between the two slopes of the ravine. Water runoff from the hills must have eroded the edges of the crevices and formed the ravine. Regardless of how it formed, we rode the roots and bounced on them as if we were riding horses. In our minds we were living in the Old West and Roy Rogers and Dale Evans riding Trigger and Buttermilk were right there with us. The dirt in this area was golden orange. Thus, the name…The Gold Mine!

We did not have a lot of official toys, but we were never at a loss for things to do. We had dolls, but mostly we played with them only when a cousin who really loved her dolls visited. Mary Ann and Janice liked to play school; I did not! They were always the teachers and I as the oldest was always the student laden with homework of my little sisters' design. Our bikes were our horses (except when we played at the gold mine) and we could ride with the wind the distance of the gravel road which was about the length of two long city blocks.

Under the shadow of migrating birds we raked walnut tree leaves on the south side of the yard although they never stayed in one pile. We made lines of leaves into house layout designs and played house within invisible walls. We dressed up in old adult-sized dresses from a trunk filled with an assortment of old clothes, which were intended to feed our imaginations, and visited each other in our houses of invisible walls. We pulled and tugged downed trees and branches to build forts in the bluffs. Dad could not have guessed what a wonderful play yard he was providing when he moved us to Dresbach.

Railroad tracks ran between our hills and the Mississippi River but the sound of the trains rumbling by did not bother us. In fact, if a train did not pass by at the usual time, we noticed it. Sometimes we had visitors who hopped trains and rode for free. Men would come across the road and up the hill to ask for handouts. Dad did not just give handouts. Knowing the value of work for a man's dignity and self-respect, he offered odd jobs like chopping wood that a man could do to earn something. Generally Mom packed a lunch and a tract with a little story or some encouraging words for the workers to take with them when they finished their jobs. If a man was willing to work with Dad, we children were to stay in the house with Mom.

Dad took action to protect Mom and provide a haven of homemade peace where the whole family would flourish. God directed us to Dresbach and over the course of the six years of living there, each of us was growing into who we were to eventually become.

CHAPTER 8

Making a Difference

"We are blessed to be a blessing." Somebody once said that and Mom and Dad took this statement seriously. They were alert to opportunities to make a difference in the lives of other people.

We saw Ben, our beekeeper neighbor, often on his knees in his garden, hunched over his strawberries, picking one long row after another. His berries were sweet, luscious, and local and sold well in corner grocery stores in La Crosse. Besides providing honey, his bees pollinated his huge field of strawberries. Though he claimed they were "friends," that "friendship" with bees did not mean he was foolish around them. On cool days when he headed to his hives to gather the honey he wore a hard hat with mesh hanging down, covering his face and neck.

Sometime after that first summer, Mom decided helping him would be the neighborly thing to do. Mary Ann and I sometimes joined her and Ben in the berry patch. We learned how to pick berries carefully and fill quart-sized balsa wood boxes to be delivered quickly to the stores. It was not work that was demanded of us, but was more like "highly suggested" as a way we could help others. For the most part being in the berry patch was fun, and popping pretty much unlimited numbers of fresh strawberries into our mouth added pleasure to the task.

Strawberry season waned just as the raspberries began to ripen. One of the chores—at least for Mary Ann and me—was to help with picking our rows and rows of raspberries. This was not as much fun as picking strawberries. Raspberry bushes had thorns. Since these bushes were a part of our garden, we *had* to pick them. Another excuse for not wanting to pick raspberries was our fear of encountering a snake. We knew there were rattlesnakes around as they outgrew their skin and shed it. If we discovered such evidence of their presence, our fear of coming across a snake multiplied. That would even be enough to dissuade us from hiking the bluffs for a while.

Mom was an early riser and would go out in the garden before we got up. One morning Mary Ann woke up early and went to find Mom in the garden. Mom was engrossed in picking raspberries and didn't notice Mary Ann sneaking up behind her with a thin stick which she brushed along Mom's leg. Mom's first thought was that it was a snake and she reacted accordingly. Mary Ann never pulled that trick again.

Weeding a specific number of rows of the garden, or picking beans and tomatoes, or husking corn were other chores for us girls. Mom often promised that if we finished our chores by a certain time, she would walk with us to the Mississippi River for a swim. We never went without her.

A swift current in the part of the Mississippi we walked to sometimes would create drop-offs. One could not be certain that the depth would be the same as it had been the previous days in any one spot. At least, that assumption was the basis of her rule at the river. We were to walk out to chest deep in the river and then swim back toward shore. In spite of that rule the swift current pulled me into its grasp one day and I was in trouble. Mom rescued me just as I was going under the water a second time and pulled me to safety.

Sometimes Dad stopped at the river on his way home from work to pick us up. If he made his appearance in his royal blue swim trunks, we knew we were in for a treat. Our swim time would be extended. He could not swim, but he would wade into the water. The kids—and not limited to just us kids—formed a crowded line. He clasped his hands together making a little platform. We stepped up into his hands and he tossed each one into the water.

The Dresbach two-room school had first, second, and third grades in the "little" room and fourth, fifth, and sixth grades in the "big" room. There was a total of six or seven kids in my age group class and a total of about twenty kids in each of the two rooms.

When the election for the school board came up, so did Dad's name. Wasn't he busy enough? Yet he decided to run for the position. He wanted to be an active participant in the education of his kids and the direction of the local school. He won the election.

Mom was a stay-at-home mom which was common during the fifties. Other than school, there were no formal or planned activities for kids in Dresbach. She saw a need for the girls in the small town to learn some homemaking skills so she started an after-school "Girl's Club" which included a Bible story with a cooking or sewing activity of the day. Mom was amazingly patient with a bunch of chatty girls messing up her kitchen.

One of the girls, Jody, who lived three or four houses from ours, came more and more often to play until she was a regular in our yard...except that she didn't have to share chores assigned to us kids. However, she repeatedly did share something else...head lice!!!

Regardless of how much Mom worked at clearing us from the infestation, it was futile. Soon the neighbor girl joined our lineup for the hair washing, vinegar treatments, combings, and checking of heads. At some point Mom finally won the battle with the lice.

We were so excited. Dad had a plan and a project. Waiting and watching while on stand-by, we would reach for any tool or part Dad requested....Anything to make the process go faster. The neighbor girl, as usual, was there watching and waiting too. At last Dad gave the word. The swing set was secured and ready for action. With an unauthorized voice of authority I announced, "Jody should go home now." I made it quite clear that just the kids in our family should have the first turns on the swings and the glider. Instead, I was the one who had to wait. I was sent into the house where I could only watch from afar and hear my siblings, plus Jody, laughing and playing.

If that incident was meant to cure me of jealousy or selfishness, it was not effective. Sharing with my siblings was not so hard, but to share with people who I felt invaded our space was a challenge for me. Clearly, Mom and Dad had kids with a sinful nature. When they needed to spank us, we knew we deserved it. They generally would preface spankings with, "This hurts me more than it hurts you." At the time we questioned that statement.

Personal time and attention from Dad was a treasure each of us savored. Janice frequently would pretend to be asleep after a trip home in the car as she knew she would be picked up in his strong arms and be carried into the house.

I cried through the fifth-grade long division problems. No one but Dad was able to have that math make sense, and even then, it did not come easily. The blessing was having Dad care enough to help me. However, when we asked how to spell a word, instead of telling us how

60

to spell it, he would just say "Look it up." Of course, his failure to give a quick answer did not look to me like he was helping. How do you look up a word if you can't spell it?

It seemed we always had other people in our home. "When can we have a family night?" was a plea we as children often made. "When can just the family be home together and have a night for popcorn and play Dirty Marbles or some other game?" One motto that became etched in the minds of at least some of us was Mom saying, "We only have this life to serve the Lord, we have an eternity to be together."

Even with so much company, running out of food was not something Mom and Dad spent time worrying about. Summer meals were the best. Beans, sliced tomatoes, or corn on the cob straight from the garden was the mainstay for summer lunches and often for suppers too. The most common and the most favorite after school snack was a big home canned dill pickle.

Since most of what was eaten was homegrown, there was much work to be done: planting, hoeing, harvesting and then came canning and freezing all that produce. Each year's harvest was our food supply intended to last until the next year's harvest. The cellar shelves would be lined with home canned garden vegetables, applesauce, dill pickles, bread and butter sweet pickles, watermelon pickles, beet pickles, jelly, and jams. Mom generally bought a bushel of peaches and some pears to can too. The freezer in the enclosed porch off the dining room would be packed with recycled waxed milk cartons filled with corn, raspberries, strawberries, sliced apples, and rhubarb. Then, there was the root cellar where things like potatoes, squash, rutabagas, onions, and beets could stay cool.

The original part of our house had a small cellar barely large enough for the shelves of canned goods. That was the only part of the house

61

with anything that resembled a basement. Through the years rooms had been added one at a time to the original house and no basement or cellar had been added under the new rooms. With all the root vegetables that needed to be stored for winter use, Dad felt we needed a root cellar.

Need is the mother of creativity, ingenuity, and a lot of hard work. Whoever had added the room beside the kitchen that Mom used as a laundry room had installed a little window in the crawl space under it. Dad removed the storm window in that crawl space. He then broke enough cement blocks of the cellar wall to create an opening that would serve as a doorway.

At first he carried the dirt up the stairs and outside until he had more room in the crawl space. Bit by bit he shoveled his way to the window. From there he shoveled dirt out through the open window. Jimmy was too young to be Dad's right-hand man so, as the oldest daughter, I filled that role. As Dad shoveled dirt out through the window, I shoveled it into a wheelbarrow. When the wheelbarrow was full or when he finished digging for the day, he backed out of the crawl space, and back out through the opening in the cement wall, reversing the way he came in. He would then take the filled wheelbarrow to the edge of the garden and dump the dirt under the weeping willow tree.

As the root cellar began to grow, so did the "hill" under the tree. This was a new place to play. We would gather a handful of the thin weeping willow branches with the long thin leaves and run, swinging out over the garden and back to the hill of dirt. It was our version of a rope swing. Of course we didn't go far but for children it was far enough to feel ourselves flying through the air. In our imaginations we were, like Tarzan, swinging from vines through the jungle.

Though we complained, we learned to have some fun in the process of work. Subtle games or goals generally hurried the work along. If the girl with dishwashing duty couldn't keep something in the rinse pan, the person drying the dishes could be excused, and the one poking along at dishwashing was required to dry the dishes too. Playing "Hangman" while doing dishes was a way to mix fun with chores, but that fill-in-the-blanks game did slow us down.

Turning over by shovel the huge garden or keeping up with weeds after working a shift on the railroad was daunting. Dad eased his workload when he bought a tiller for the garden. He wore a white tank top undershirt and pants (rarely did he wear shorts at that time) and got behind the tiller. His face and arms not covered by his undershirt would turn red, and beads of sweat dripped off his face. He did not complain of sunburn or sweat stinging his eyes. He simply knew what needed to be done and set to work.

The guests saw only a plate of corn and potatoes and all the trimmings but we saw Dad sweating at the workload to provide not only for the family he was responsible for, but for those he and Mom chose to bless through their hospitality and generosity.

Whether it was beans, tomatoes, corn, or cucumbers, the first of the season crops were shared with the Anderson family. Dad and Mom explained that the firstfruits belong to the Lord and giving to the pastor was one way of giving to the Lord. However, their giving extended beyond the gift of the first of the crops. Often during the summers when we went to La Crosse, we would take a bushel of tomatoes or corn, or whatever was in season, to the pastor's wife so she could can or freeze food too.

The church was small and offerings generally matched the size of the congregation. Pastor Anderson felt that the bills for the church needed to be paid first. If there was money left, he would then take his salary. It was of greater importance to him to maintain the testimony of church and not be late in paying the church bills. Since Dad was on the church board, he knew Pastor's conviction and Dad respected him for that. Dad and Mom repeatedly expressed joy in having a harvest to share with them.

An aunt and uncle and their two girls came from Minneapolis during harvest time every year for corn. After tucking us cousins into bed, we would fall asleep listening to the adults laughing and joking as they worked into the night husking or freezing corn. When the city family packed up to go home, they would take fresh and frozen corn with them. There was a trade of sorts; they brought clothes my cousins had outgrown for us girls.

Dad never complained about work. Instead, work was just what occupied each day. There didn't seem to be a division between work and recreation. Life was just giving yourself to the thing at hand to be done. We saw the effects of hard labor on his body (like his red face dripping with sweat when he tilled the garden or the groan when he would swing the ax to chop wood for the kitchen stove, etc.). But we also saw him demonstrating an attitude of enjoyment while he labored. Work was not synonymous with something negative. A good work ethic was something he was raised with. His mother even wrote in my autograph book, "Whatever your hand findeth to do, do it with thy might" (Ecclesiastes 9:10a). This was the wisdom she wanted to share with the next generation. Good work ethics characterized the McDowell family. This was more caught (by example) than taught.

After we had lived in Dresbach for about four years a newly appointed pastor came to serve the Methodist church there. He actually lived in a nearby town and divided his time between three churches of the three small towns in the area. The Dresbach Methodist church was one of the three. This new pastor understood that salvation through trusting Jesus as Savior is the only way to have sin forgiven and the only hope for eternal life. He heard about Mom and the Girls' Club so he visited us and asked Mom and Dad if they would participate with him in teaching in the church.

After praying about it, Dad and Mom agreed that Mom would teach and we would attend summer vacation Bible school in Dresbach as well as in La Crosse. Dad and Mom had wanted to reach out to the community when they moved there and now with this invitation by the local pastor, the right time had come. God opened that door.

A certain man and his wife in Dresbach had become believers. They had seven children and their income depended on how much snowplowing or highway weed cutting needed to be done each season. Mom and Dad befriended them and invited them into our home often.

It was during that time that Dad would stop after work some days at a bakery in La Crosse that sold day-old goods. If we saw Dad carrying one of those brown emptied fifty-pound size flour bags in from the car, we would come running. It was like Christmas! We didn't know what bakery surprises there might be inside those big brown bags. It was ho hum if the bag only contained bread or rolls, but sometimes there were day-old doughnuts or pastries. This mystery bag of baked goods cost a dollar. Dad frequently bought one bag for us and one for this family they had befriended. Though Mom made homemade bread we—at least us kids—considered it a treat to get store-bought bread.

Mom had the opportunity to attend a first-aid class in Winona. Dresbach had no medical resources so, for any medical needs, a person would have to make a ten-mile trip to either La Crosse or ten miles in the other direction to Winona. The idea of learning how to be better prepared to care for family or neighbors motivated her, even though taking these classes meant a ten-mile round trip for Mom to drive alone, in the dark, and on the two-lane highway. This class was offered a few years after we had moved to Dresbach and by then Mom had learned to drive.

She had opportunities to use what she learned in the classes. One night coming home from class she came upon the scene of an accident. Mom stopped to help and she was able to put into practice what she had just learned that night.

Once when the family with seven kids was at our house, their little girl stopped breathing. Mom did what she was taught. Amazingly, the girl started breathing and the parents rushed her to the hospital in La Crosse while we took care of the rest of the kids. Shortly after this, that family moved to Arizona for the sake of their asthmatic daughter.

Minnesota social services made known their need for more foster families. The number of children in the state system needing care greatly outnumbered caregivers willing to be or able to qualify as foster care providers. Mom and Dad felt this would be something they could do, so almost as soon as our family was approved by the state, two-year-old Marty Lynn arrived with little more than a stuffed toy with a wind-up music box inside it. She was easily recognized as being developmentally slow both mentally and physically. We loved her. Other girls had dolls to shower love and care on but we had a real baby. She needed more mothering than most children her age but between Janice and me, and especially Mary Ann, and of course Mom, Marty Lynn had all the care she needed in order to thrive in our home during the two years she was a part of our family.

When the day came for our foster girl to leave our family our hearts were breaking. Mom and Dad made arrangements with the foster care worker to come for her while we four kids were in school. Dad and Mom tried their best to protect us as much as they could from such painful things in life like saying good-bye to Marty Lynn. She was loved and she seemed to know it. Years later Mom and Dad again became licensed in Wisconsin and took in at least three more foster children until those children could be returned to their parents.

We saw Mom and Dad's generosity with their time and resources. They involved us kids sometimes more than what we would have chosen, but they did not ask of us more than what they lived out by their example. They not only told us, but they showed us that we are blessed to be a blessing.

CHAPTER 9

JIMMY BOY

It was perfectly okay with us to become owners of Patsy the day we moved to Dresbach. Jimmy, the lone boy in this family of girls, was delighted with this new friend. He would crawl right into Patsy's doghouse literally and figuratively. He could get himself into trouble and get himself out of it and all the while be entertaining. Uncle Hugh had a reel-to-reel movie camera. He recorded Jimmy crawling in and out of the doghouse with a "look what I can do" grin on his face as he emerged.

Jimmy was about two years old when, as newcomers in the neighborhood, our family visited our elderly neighbors, Mr. and Mrs. Moore. Mr. Moore was a veteran with a collection of military memorabilia which included an old gun. Jimmy had never been exposed to guns or even TV westerns since there was no TV in our home at the time. Yet, he picked up that gun and held it as if he knew how to handle one. The veteran was clearly amused with the little neighbor boy who showed a mutual interest. (Little did we know at that time Jimmy would grow up to be a policeman.)

Jimmy liked to lurk on the sofa in wait for one of his sisters to walk by. One lunge and he would drag one of us down to the floor and wrestle with us. Invariability a girl's cry for help would bring Mom to the rescue. She would often deflect the crisis by saying, "You want to fight? Put up your dukes," and she would put her fists out and take a boxing stance. Mother and son would have a little pretend boxing match until the laughing brought the "conflict" to a halt.

Mom would often say she didn't know what to do with boys. The training methods for the girls just didn't work with Jimmy. The form of discipline Mom most often resorted to was having him sit on a stool in the kitchen where she could keep an eye on him—sort of as a time out with a promise of a spanking when Dad got home.

It did not prove to be much of a discipline measure. Jimmy found that he could loop his belt around the rim of the stool and "rock 'n' ride" his stool all around the kitchen. Yes, he obeyed by staying on the stool, but he certainly was not confined to the point of suffering for his wrong action. Still, Mom could see that he was not getting into something else he shouldn't be doing.

A frequent question when Dad arrived home was "How many spankings tonight?" Those spankings were not handed out with emotions of anger. Dad's usual comment preceding spankings was "This hurts me more than it hurts you." When we were not the ones on the receiving end of the spankings, it was easier to see what he claimed was true.

This was one point of disagreement between Mom and Dad. Dad felt he should not be the one to apply the "board of education" all the time. But Mom's other options didn't seem to have much corrective effect. Their discussions about differing opinions were not in the presence of the children, however. To us four kids it seemed that Mom and Dad were unified in their expectations and in agreement regarding consequences of unacceptable behavior.

They had established earlier in their marriage that they would not go to sleep angry with each other. Mom later shared with her girls that when she would crawl into bed and turn her back to Dad, he insisted they talk it out before they could go to sleep. Not that they could solve every problem before going to sleep, but they would not go to sleep with the problem coming between them. The problem may not be resolved, but the goal was for them to be united against the problem. These kinds of discussions would be dealt with but not in the presence of us children. We did not observe how they talked through the issues or how resolutions to conflicts can be worked out. We would have to learn that on our own.

Did Jimmy deserve all those spankings? It certainly seemed so at the time! Jimmy was innocently creative in finding new actions that certainly were not supposed to be repeated. One day Mom had just finished vacuuming the soot from the oil space burner furnace in the living room. She had the kind of vacuum cleaner with a bag that had to be emptied before it could be returned to its place in the vacuum and be used again. She had emptied that soot onto newspapers and rolled up the paper to confine the soot. When she left the room, Jimmy took the newspaper and shook it…and shook it some more. Puffs of black soot settled all over Jimmy and the living room.

Another time Jimmy and Sammy, his neighborhood friend, decided to chop down a sapling. Apparently he felt there was no advantage in checking it out with Mom for her approval. Jimmy thought he knew how. He had watched Dad and he knew where the ax was kept. What else was there to know? What Jimmy had not observed were safety precautions and a few details that would make the job easier. Jimmy swung the ax and the sapling bounced. "Hold it, Sammy." So Sammy took hold of the sticklike tree, and Jimmy took a swing again...a little too close to where Sammy was holding it. The story related through the years is that Sammy almost lost a finger that day.

Sometimes things Jimmy did were accidents within the scope of just being a boy and no discipline was warranted. For example, Jimmy loved to climb the catalpa tree in the front yard. Dad set up a cement block so Jimmy could reach the first branch. Trees are nature's Jungle gym. It was part of the wonderful country playground we grew up enjoying. But one day Jimmy fell from that tree. The top of his head hit the block, leaving a deep gash. Mom examined the wound as she held his head under the faucet, washing away the blood. I was "helping" Mom and I peeked too into the split in his head. All my "helping" made me worse than useless. A neighbor arrived to drive Mom and Jimmy to the doctor in La Crosse. No way was I in any condition to stay with Mary Ann and Janice after my trauma of seeing blood and looking into the gap in Jimmy's scalp, so a neighbor lady watched over my sisters and I made the trip to the doctor with Mom and Jimmy. The doctor stitched up his head and the wound healed without further problems.

Other than for such emergencies, going to the doctor was a rare thing. In those days we only went if we were really sick or if we needed shots for getting into school. Fevers, flu, and colds were treated at home. Jimmy became sick and he had a high temperature the summer after he finished first grade. His fever did not respond to Mom's home treatments like they normally would.

"Jimmy, what's wrong with you?" Mom was in tears. Jimmy was seeing things and saying things that made no sense. This was beyond anything Mom and Dad knew how to deal with. The doctor hospitalized Jimmy at once with the diagnosis of encephalitis, a disease spread by infected mosquitoes. The doctor had seen other cases that summer and the outcomes were not good. Jimmy went into a coma and life changed for all of us.

When one family member suffers, all suffer. Mom and Dad stayed in La Crosse at the hospital with Jimmy. When Dad had to be at work Mom stayed beside Jimmy. Our five single McDowell aunts, who loved and cared about each of their nieces and nephews, stepped up to the plate to help care for us girls. After some time of Mom's constant presence at Jimmy's side, the doctor ordered her to go home and get some sleep. When she finally gave in to that order, Aunt Etta was the one Mom trusted to stay beside Jimmy while she slept.

While all this was going on, Janice had her own personal crisis. Would anybody even remember her birthday? Of course Mom and Dad remembered, but their focus was on the crisis at the hospital. However, the McDowell aunts were also well aware of her birthday and they made it a memorable event for Janice. They baked a 9 x 13-inch cake, cut it up like puzzle pieces, and arranged the pieces together to form the shape of a butterfly. Aunt Elsie—so typical of her attention to detail and decorations—bought all the extra candies indicated in the cake decorating guide to make it look just like the picture. Then, wrapped up in a beautiful package, was a store-bought dress—chosen special for her, and not a hand-me-down from her older sisters. No, Janice was not forgotten. The cake and gift spoke volumes to one little girl who needed to know that her birthday was still important even in the middle of Jimmy's hospitalization.

Mom and Dad were dealing with the biggest crisis they had ever faced. The doctor said "If"—and that was a big if. "*If* Jimmy comes out of the coma, he will be a vegetable or at best be handicapped in some way." Of course, the "'Why, God?" question was asked, Of course, there were tears and prayers, many prayers. Pastor Anderson and others came to the hospital to support and pray with Mom and Dad. Jimmy did wake up but a couple days later lapsed back into a coma. One aunt in Amery was out in the hayfield on the farm and had the sudden burden to stop haying right there in the middle of that process and pray for Jimmy. Later we learned this happened at the critical timing of Jimmy lapsing into his second coma.

Mom and Dad were trusting the Lord and praying for a miracle. They knew God has the power to heal. They knew God is wise and is in control even when we might question what He is doing. They struggled but finally, surrendering Jimmy to the Lord, they prayed, "Not our will, but Thine be done. Dear Lord, we surrender him to You. We again dedicate our son, this son we waited for so long, this son who is such a challenge, and yet who brings so much joy and laughter to us and so many others. Lord, we give him to You."

It was a long time of wondering if Jimmy would live or die; a long time to be in the waiting room of not knowing, of trusting God while they could not see beyond the dark shadows of this valley. But God did wake him up! He had a hearing challenge for a while in one ear, and he had to repeat first grade as he had forgotten the lessons of that year. He also had an anger problem that was a new side to his personality which was probably related to frustration. But he was as much Jimmy Boy after his illness as he was before.

Waiting for him at home was his dog, Pal. (Patsy had been hit by a car some time before this event.) Pal had not forgotten Jimmy, and Jimmy had not forgotten Pal. When anger surfaced, Jimmy and Pal would take off for the bluffs behind our house. Years later, Jim credited God for freeing him from that anger.

Yes, God did bring healing. But before He did, Mom and Dad yielded their son and their will to the Lord. God could say no just as easily as He could answer with a yes. "Thy will be done on earth as it is in heaven" were not words lightly spoken. They had struggled, but when they prayed these words, they fully felt the meaning of what they were saying. Dad and Mom experienced God in new ways through Jimmy's illness. They also learned how very much it means to be supported in prayer by so many people. "The effectual fervent prayer of a righteous man availeth much." Those words from James 5:16 would from that time on be associated with Jimmy's illness...and his recovery.

CHAPTER 10

A LITTLE SURPRISE

We lived between the bluffs on one side of our house and a bank that sloped down to the level of the Old Highway 61 on the other side. From there the landscape dipped even lower to the railroad tracks and the shoreline of the Mississippi River. Life is like that—hills and valleys even through changing seasons—and life goes on. For six years we had been living generally on the hilly side of life, but change was coming. So was the heavy road equipment.

Plans were finalized for the next stretch of the new highway, and our living room was right in the path of what was to be crushed and bulldozed aside. Our woods and the hills would be blasted to make a level path for what most people called progress. Our gravel road, the raspberry bushes, and the rich soil of Mom's neatly tended garden would be scraped clean and covered over with a mesh of rebar and solidified with thick layers of cold cement. We knew that was coming.

Some neighbors had houses that could be moved back a distance from the path of the new highway. Ours could not. Since it had been built one section at a time it would crumble if moved.

Mom again was troubled. "Hormones?" she questioned. The change of life was surely upon her. Now at almost 40 years of age she was experiencing changes in her body that were not expected, yet could not be denied.

"No," the doctor surprised her. "These changes have nothing to do with your age!"

For Mom, the attitude was, "Oh no! I don't feel like starting over with a baby." But to Mary Ann, Janice, and me, nothing could have brought more excitement than the anticipation of a new baby in the family. A baby who would not, like Marty Lynn, be a "borrowed for a while" foster child family member.

It had to be a time of challenge on several fronts for Dad. He had an almost 40-year-old pregnant wife who was not happy to be in this condition. His kids understood only that their home, school, playground in the hills, and just about everything in their lives would be changing. Dad was dealing with how much in resources the state would offer for our property and where he would move his growing family.

Mom and Dad looked at lots of country homes since the country seemed to be the place where the family had thrived, but nothing was right about any of the places realtors showed them. Both the June date set by the state of Minnesota for vacating the Dresbach property and the delivery date for baby number five inched closer. A decision had to be made. La Crosse had more properties on the market that fit their housing needs than anything they could find in the surrounding countryside.

It was settled. We would move back to Market Street in La Crosse just a few blocks from the house we had lived in six years before. The house we would move to had been owned by only one family though it was sixty-one years old. There was much about it that was beautiful, especially to those who love character and the antique look. The appeal for our family was the four bedrooms and lots of space for a still growing family, plus the fact that Dad's offer on the house was accepted.

Like every other house we had looked at, this one too was not perfect. The only bathroom was on the second floor with the bedrooms—not exactly ideal for Mom's pregnant condition. She was well into the nesting stage when we moved in. By July the move was behind us, and our attention turned toward preparing in earnest for the new baby.

Dad and Mom had the large bedroom at the top of the stairs. Some nights we gathered there for evening devotions. Our very tired mom would lie in bed while we knelt beside it. By the time we finished praying, the baby would often be making his presence known by kicking and Mom's nightgown moved with every kick. We were bonding with that baby. The excitement of us girls had added to Mom's acceptance and, eventually, even her eagerness for the arrival of this baby (or perhaps for her return to a non-pregnant body).

A family from church lived nearby and hosted a surprise baby shower. We successfully kept it a secret. Dad took Mom out, using some excuse he had come up with. As soon as they left the house, we finished washing the dishes and scooted over to the Taylors' house.

The guests and all four of us kids were waiting quietly when Dad knocked on the door. Mom saw us kids first and started scolding us for sneaking over to the neighbor's house. Obviously, she was surprised because she would not have scolded us had she known the real reason for us being there. Mary Ann, Janice, and I were more excited about all the little baby gifts than Mom, I think.

The big gift of the party was a changing table with a plastic bathtub under the table. That would be placed in the kitchen where most of the family activity took place. This baby would be the center of our attention.

In 1961 the sign with the hospital rules hung where it could not be ignored—one rule glaringly apparent: "No one under the age of sixteen allowed on the maternity floor." I was less than four months from qualifying for visiting and I certainly could pass for being sixteen. But, rules are rules. Unlike some, Dad felt that rules are *not* made to be broken, no matter how anxious I was to see our new brother.

Dad surprised us though. He did feel okay about us using the stairwell to climb up to the maternity floor. Without any of us kids taking one step onto the maternity floor, he opened the stairway door and whispered while he pointed, "That's Mom's room." A nurse carried a baby into the room. That was the first peek we had of Timothy.

When Dad drove home with a very tired wife and new baby, three girls were waiting with arms eager to hold their new brother. We kissed his toes and wondered about his long fingers that were surely destined for playing the piano. He had a cowlick that made an outline of a heart within the frizz of hair on the back of his head. We four kids were convinced that all the love we had poured into him showed up in his cowlick as if that heart was showing his love for us too.

We had been surrounded with examples of loving and caring for babies by Mom and Dad and the whole McDowell family. By the time Tim was born there had been a bunch of cousins born into the family. Since Mary Ann and I were two of the oldest ones, we had been a part of the hands welcoming new cousins. I took turns in the church nursery as often as I had the chance. Mary Ann and I were prepared by example and practice to pitch in for every phase of the baby's care…even the middle of the night bottle feedings.

Though the family moved from the hills of the country to the streets of the city, life would continue to be lived, as most lives are, between the hills and the valleys. We were beginning to adjust to a new kind of normal again on Market Street, this time as a family of seven.

Back row: Jim, Stella, Mary Ann, and Janice.
Front row: Dad, Tim, and Mom

CHAPTER 11

Teenagers

Dad might talk things over with someone, but he was not one to give speeches. Even as a teen I do not remember getting lectures from my parents. Life lessons were more caught than taught. Generally Dad just lived his convictions without realizing the impact he was having on those around him. Family devotions, attending Sunday school, church, and Wednesday night prayer meetings were the established pattern in our home. How Mom and Dad lived daily was consistent with what they believed.

When I was in junior high we were still living in Dresbach. Each school day the junior and senior high school kids would be bused to La Crosse for school. The transition from the two-room elementary school to the city junior high was not going well. I thought to be accepted I would try to act like my peers, but that was not within my comfort zone. So I retreated to being alone, especially over the lunch time. My parents could not help but be aware of my struggles.

Aunt Alida and Uncle Reo lived about six blocks from my school with their young son and new baby girl. Mom asked Alida if she would be willing to have me walk to their house and have lunch with them. That was such a perfect answer to my loneliness. I clearly was a McDowell if loving and caring for babies was any indication. In the middle of my very hard days I had an oasis—a place to go and a purpose. The walk refreshed and energized me while feeding or even diapering a baby gave me a sense of belonging and being needed, and what young teen doesn't need that?

I would sometimes walk the few blocks after school in the opposite direction from my midday oasis to Aunts Etta and Jenny's apartment. Dad would pick me up there when he finished work and we would ride home to Dresbach together. One day I arrived at their apartment, went in the backdoor as usual to the kitchen, and was told to stay there. "You can start your homework at the kitchen table today," I was hurriedly told before my aunt turned to go into the next rooms. Something must be wrong. This certainly was not the usual greeting I received.

My Grandma McDowell had been very sick. She and Grandpa had been staying in La Crosse at the aunts' place where they would be closer to the La Crosse doctors Grandma had been seeing. People were using the front door which was highly unusual. I could hear muffled familiar voices from the front room where I knew Grandma was in a hospital bed. Dad arrived from work and he also went straight into the front room. Still nothing was said to me of what was going on. I could not focus on my homework. Something really was wrong...nothing was normal this day and I could only wonder why.

The phone rang. Aunt Etta came out to the kitchen to answer it. "No, we will not be coming tonight." Etta's lips and her voice quivered, "We just lost Mother."

What? Grandma McDowell had died? It was the first time anyone that close to me had died. I left the schoolwork at the table and inched

84

closer to the edge of the kitchen door where the muffled voices were now a little clearer. Dad was speaking. His voice was steady, given the situation. As the oldest son, it seemed that the role of servant leadership fell on him. As children, when Dad's parents had to be away for some reason, their instruction was for the younger ones to mind Etta and Fritz. It was natural for them now in this time of so many what-to-do-next decisions to look to my dad as well as to Grandpa. Words were not clearly heard from my spot at the kitchen door but I knew their voices. Was there another voice too? Perhaps the doctor had come?

By the time Dad emerged from the front room and was ready to head toward Dresbach, it was dark outside. He had remained strong for what he needed to do to help his family. Not until after the two of us were in the car headed home did I see him cry. He may have cried in the front room with his family, but this was the first time I remember seeing my dad cry.

So that's how you deal with death, I observed. You set aside your feelings, and do what you need to do so you can be helpful in the situation. There would be a time and place for you to mourn later. Dad was simply living life as he knew he needed to, and his example taught me an invaluable lesson he never intended to teach that day. (Neither of us knew at the time that I would become a nurse and how valuable this lesson would be for me.)

Much later Grandpa needed care at a hospital located about three blocks from my La Crosse junior high-school. Grandpa McDowell had earned a reputation as a stubborn noncompliant patient. He was used to being in charge and giving orders, so he did not handle taking orders well. One way he opposed the staff was his refusal to eat, which was vital for his diabetic condition. Dad and his siblings had done what they could to help him, and having done all they could, somebody brought

85

idea that maybe I could get him to eat. So, while he was hospitalized I would walk to the hospital during my lunch hour and feed him. He would not oppose his first grandchild like he was doing with the hospital staff. I chatted away as I put each spoonful into his mouth. His eyes were set on me and all my antics as I talked and he ate. My teenage sense of value soared, knowing I was a part of the adult McDowell team working together to solve problems. What a blessing to have an important part in caring for my grandpa.

It was always much easier to fit in with the family than with my peers. The kids already in the youth group groaned with the start of each new school year when the *little* kids in seventh grade walked into the group feeling much more grown up than they really were. But, seventh grade was the rite of passage into the teen years whether seventh graders were welcomed or not.

Junior High Bible Camp was really the introduction into the church youth group. There was a big cost involved in sending a child for the week. People often asked, "Fritz, how can you afford to send all your kids to camp." Dad's response was that he couldn't afford to have them *not* go.

Camp was the place where I made the decision that I would not compromise my standards in order to be accepted by classmates who did not share my values. I would choose Jesus as my Friend even if He would be the only friend I would have in school. I was challenged to carry my Bible to school. Reading my Bible during the ten mile bus ride to school gave me help and hope for the days. Psalms 46:1 became my verse during those difficult days. "The Lord is my refuge and strength; A very present help in trouble." Seeing it on top of my armload of textbooks through the day was a reminder that Jesus was with me. Another difference it made for me was to consider my actions. I did not

86

want to bring disgrace on Him by doing anything that would dishonor Him. I made this decision the summer between seventh and eighth grade and I carried my Bible from that year on until I graduated from high school. This decision I made at Bible camp set my course for the rest of my junior and senior high school years.

Dad became so convinced of the importance of camp in the lives of his kids that he graduated from just paying the way for sending his own kids to really getting involved. A group of area churches rented a campground for two weeks for their young people. Later when the camp was not available for rent for even those two weeks, some pastors and parents who had seen the value of Bible camp started dreaming of buying property and developing Arrowhead Bible Camp. Dad was fully on board with this vision. He and others prayed and put their time and energies into that vision until it became a reality. It was small, so small, at first but over the years it would grow. (As of this writing the camp has had an impact on the lives and futures of over five hundred children and youth during the summer of 2015 alone.)

Mom and Dad knew the friends we associated with and most of their parents. The church youth group often came to our home, mostly for singing around the piano or playing games after the evening service and for food...always food. Pizza was a fairly new food in our lives, but it was the teen treat of choice. If there were pizza parlors then, we had not been introduced to them. Our pizza came from the Chef Boyardee yellow box. Each box contained a packet of the dry ingredients for the crust, a small can of sauce, and a packet of cheese. Even coming from a box, it took time to make it. As teenagers we learned to like it because pizza was growing in popularity. Dad did not claim a fondness for it for a long time. He said, "Oh, I like it all right. It just doesn't like me."

Every quarter the youth from our church met for larger youth gatherings that included several area churches. Those events included a fun activity, a devotional, and a lot of interaction and food. Since the churches were some distance apart, each church group would ride to the event together and then kids would pair up with special friends or prearranged dates from other churches.

For these quarterly youth functions, drivers were needed for hauling kids if they could not all fit into the pastor's car. Generally the older boys, fresh behind the wheel, took advantage of opportunities to drive and be the "big man" with a car. Given the chance, they would rev up the motors or revamp the muffler on the car to get an edge on attracting attention. Sometimes dads wisely volunteered to fill in as drivers.

When Dad drove the kids to those youth meetings, just his presence in the background was reassuring. This was not the attitude most kids expressed to their peers when their fathers were present. Busy as he was, choosing to help out with driving made a statement of his involvement in the lives of his girls. Though he never came across as a powerhouse or threat, just knowing that a girl's father was active in his daughters' lives had to have an influence on how boys would treat his girls. It certainly had an influence on us as we each treasured personal time and attention from our father.

One of the first quarterly activities for the area churches I went to was bowling. I had not found friends yet in the group so my bowling partner was Dad (who really was just who I wanted to have one-on-one time with). I had no knowledge of the game except it was expensive. After getting a couple gutter balls on my first two turns, I pleaded with Dad, "We don't have to do this. I'm no good at this and it's too expensive." I thought you had to pay the fee every time you rolled the ball down the alley (or in my case, the gutter). I had watched how hard Dad worked and did not want him to waste his money. "I would rather just not bowl." Dad chuckled and reassured me that I could roll the ball several more times without having to pay more.

Mom and Dad never sat us girls down and told us the rules for dating. We were confident of Mom and Dad's love and best interests for us. We knew by parental example and by the things they valued what the family standards were. We had a desire to please our parents…and many decisions we as teens made were easier because family values were very clear.

Jim remembered one of Dad's short speeches. "Dad pulled me aside when I was in high school and said, 'Jim, if you ever came home drunk, you would break your mother's heart.'" That was all Dad said. Jim chose not to drink. He was a star player on the football and basketball varsity teams in high school, but he said that shooting baskets with Dad became for him a special memory of his high school years.

Dad and Mom would not hold on tightly to their children when the time came for us to marry. They always said I was their practice child. So when I was about to get married, patterns emerged regarding the process of officially launching their children.

As each of us approached marriage, the whole family became well acquainted with the one who would be joining the family. Dad and Mom made it clear that when we married, the mate would become a part of our family and we would be expected to become a part of our mate's family. The new couple would not be isolated—out there alone—but would be an extension of our McDowell family. The couple would not be under their rule though. Mom and Dad would be there for hugs and encouragement and for wise counsel worthy to be considered but never would their words come across with an authoritative "you must do this" kind of delivery.

As each of us married, we could always count on Mom and Dad

for prayer and emotional support. However, they made it clear that we were not to come running home with packed bags because of trouble or discord in our marriage. Each couple would be expected to persevere in working out the problems between them. This advice was a surprise.

Sometimes their conversations would end with Mom addressing Dad as "Mr. Right" but those conversations did not look or sound like fights. This does not mean there were never expressed differences of opinions. One time I observed Mom crying because a trip to visit her parents had to be canceled and she was disappointed but she was not using tears to get her way. Though Dad characteristically kept his promises he was also guided by wisdom and common sense. If he had to say no, it was because there was a good reason for that decision. None of us could remember seeing Mom and Dad having a fight so a real conflict in marriage was not something expected, nor had we seen by their example how to deal with or resolve major marital disagreements.

In giving his daughter to a husband, Dad also was giving the new husband the responsibility of providing for his bride's needs. Mary Ann, Janice, and I were not in the habit of making great demands for extra frills some girls sought for. We had pretty much learned to be content or even thrive with what was provided. That attitude would also continue in the future, but the husband was to be responsible financially once a couple married.

By the time Dad walked me down the aisle, he had already filled the role of father of the bride for two other young women who had looked to him as their father figure for this special day in their lives. (That number would continue to grow even after Dad had given all three of us girls away. When asked recently how many times Dad had filled in for the father of the bride role, Mom said she had lost count.)

Terry and I married during the time I was still finishing nurses' training so the remaining schooling expenses would belong to us. Together we were to learn how to manage our finances. That letting go of the "little ones" to fly on their own is a commitment to tough love. Yes, it might be easier for parents to step in and make life easier for a young couple, but Mom and Dad held the conviction that generally there is long-term benefit for a couple to learn to work together through the challenges of making life work for them. This is similar to how the process of transformation within a chrysalis, plus the struggle a butterfly experiences when emerging from it, equips and strengthens it for a new life.

Dad and Mom had done their part in training their children and now the four oldest kids would be testimonies of their labor and love for a whole new generation. Still, they were not done with the training process.

Tim was not yet three years old when I got married so Dad and Mom still had a long road of parenting ahead. Tim was not like Mary Ann, Janice, or me, and not even like Jim. Tim had his own kind of challenges for Mom and Dad that they would never have imagined. Some of his choices would break their hearts. But, neither did they know some of the joys and the motivation he would provide…especially for Mom in coming days.

Stella's wedding was the first time he would walk one of his own daughters down the aisle.

CHAPTER 12

THE ACCIDENT

Dad answered the phone.

"Fritz McDowell?"

Dad acknowledged that yes, this was he.

The voice continued. "Your wife and her three passengers have been in a car accident near Chippewa Falls. You need to come."

Pastor Lee Weiss, the pastor at that time, Dale Wagner from church, and Dad quickly arranged care for their kids before the three men piled into one car for a somber almost one-hundred-mile trip to the Chippewa Falls hospital.

Their wives—Joann Weiss, Joyce Wagner—Mae and an elderly widow, Sadie, had been returning from the district area women's meeting in Eau Claire, Wisconsin. An oncoming truck on the opposite side of the highway divider lost control and hit a car in front of him. The truck driver then crossed the highway divider and hit Mom's car which swung around and was hit again by the truck. The load of barn stanchions he was hauling shifted and rolled onto Mom's car. Like most accidents, the crunching and crashing of metal happened in a flash of time. Details would gradually be sorted out by the experts, but later it was proven that

Mom was not at fault.

The four women were still in their seat belts and pinned in the car. Mom called out to each of her passengers by name and they each moaned a response. Paramedics arrived. As they worked to get the others out, she heard them talking. "If we could just get the driver out…she's in the worse shape." Though pain pulsed throughout her body, she was comforted to know that if she was identified as being hurt the most, then the others must be in better condition than she was.

Ambulances had already rushed the others to the Chippewa Falls hospital before Mom could be extracted from the tangled metal. One leg was broken, and her ribs were crushed from the pressure of the steering wheel. The impact to her face had been so severe that her nose had been crushed too. She appeared to have little left of a nose.

The three men arrived at the Chippewa Falls hospital together in their one car. Dale was taken to his wife, Joyce. Her back was broken and she would be taken to surgery. Pastor Lee was taken to another area to be told that his wife, Joann, had died though they had done everything they could. There was no family for Sadie, but the men were told that she too had died.

But where was Mom? Her injuries required the care of specialty doctors so she was flown to one of the two Eau Claire, Wisconsin, hospitals since the Chippewa hospital had no eye, ear, and nose specialist.

With only one car between the three men, Dad waited with Lee until everything that needed to be done immediately was completed. Dale would stay at the Chippewa hospital with his wife. Then Dad and Lee drove to Eau Claire.

It was about 11 p.m. before the two men arrived. The nurse asked about the condition of the others. From her room Mom recognized

Pastor's voice saying, "My wife and an older lady from the church did not survive. The other lady is in surgery in the Chippewa Falls hospital." Mom's heart sank. She hoped she would die before they walked into her room. How could she face Pastor Lee? She had been the driver.

Lee and Joann Weiss were like Mom and Dad's own kids, and like grandparents to the Weiss children. Those four young children were frequently at the house while Joann and Lee had ministry obligations. How could Mom face the children who no longer had a mother? How could she look into Lee's eyes? She silently cried out to the Lord, "Take me now before I have to face Lee."

In spite of his sorrow, Lee had a weak smile as he came into the room. "I'm so sorry, Lee," Mom said. "I heard what you said about Joann."

The pastor looked at Mom's face which was difficult to view. Her nose had been crushed and pushed inward. Dad could not hide his emotions. The room was heavy with sorrow, yet Lee gently touched Mom's hand and whispered, "Joann's better off. She's not suffering. She's with the Lord." This was not an "I hope so" kind of faith. They each knew from God's Word that what Lee had said was true.

"But you…and the children…with Joann gone…" Mom started to say. It was a sentence that didn't need to be finished. It was a time of faith overcoming the realities of the events of that August 26, 1972, day. Faith did not take away the pain of loss and grief. But faith that God was still in control was a comfort.

Family members got calls. Mary Ann and Gil were in Mundelein, Illinois. Janice was in college in the Twin Cities not far from Terry and me and our three children. She canceled her first date with Dave and went to Eau Claire instead. Terry and I packed up our kids in the Volkswagen van and headed to the hospital. Visiting rules prohibited the children from visiting their grandma so someone always stayed in or near the van with them while the adults took turns with Mom.

While Dad was taking his turn with the grandchildren, a bee or wasp found its way into the van. The children who had not grown up with bees in Dresbach panicked, but Dad calmly killed the intruder with his bare hands. Even in the crisis of those days, Dad was the protector for his family as much as he was able. In simply doing what he could, he became a hero to one grandson. Even as an adult, this grandson recalled this event as one of many favorite memories of his grandpa caring for him.

Over the next few weeks various visitors came and went. Sorrow, guilt, and pain were especially oppressive visitors during the nights, but God was also revealing His presence. Of all the rooms she could have been assigned to in the Eau Claire hospital, Mom had a room with a view. From her pillow she could see the glow of a lighted cross. To Mom it was a visible reminder of God's presence. He had not abandoned her. He who was also acquainted with sorrow and pain was there in the midst of her blackest times. No one understood like Jesus.

Another visitor shared, "With God there is no such word as 'accident'. In His eyes this was an incident in life. Though we cannot understand the whys, God knows, and He still has a good plan. Someday we will know…maybe in this life, maybe not until we reach heaven. Even this, we will see, is part of how He is working all things together for good for those who love Him and are called according to His purpose." The visitor was referring to Romans 8:28.

Sometimes in the middle of such sorrow it may seem insensitive to say such things. But these words did not originate in the thoughts of man, but with God. Visitors who shared Scriptures with Mom during those difficult days brought words that addressed so many of the issues she was struggling with. Waves of sorrow and self-imposed guilt hit her like breakers crashing onto a rugged shoreline. Two little words from Psalms 37— "Fret not" and "Fret not" and repeated a third time "Fret not"—came to her over and over. Those simple words became a weapon against depressive and destructive self-condemnation thoughts. God's Word, His truth, brought comfort, hope, and a growing understanding that God is still in control. Our days are in His hands to do with according to His will. Not that we can always understand, but that's where trust in God is fleshed out in day-by-day living.

Dad, the protector and provider for his family, had challenges too. Now he was the one to see that someone was at home to care for 11-year-old Tim while Jim, as a high school senior, could take more responsibility for himself. Dad also needed to be there for Mom in Eau Claire and then later in La Crosse when she was well enough to be transferred to a hospital closer to home.

Though he had a good sense of business matters, dealing with insurance and accident related legal issues were all new to him. Insurance and legal representatives tried to stir up division between the families and bring the blame game into the picture. But Lee, Dad, and Dale stayed firm in their unity as brothers in Christ and in their care and concern for one another. Each of them had to make decisions and make plans they had not prepared for.

Joann's funeral and burial were near her hometown and family. Ladies from the La Crosse church tried to fill in, caring for the children and helping out with housekeeping. That was not a good solution. Next Lee brought in one of the older widows from the church as a full-time housekeeper/nanny. That also was not the answer the family needed. Where was God's answer to the children's and Lee's needs? How could he, as a single father, continue the demands of shepherding a whole congregation plus juggle the responsibilities of his now very needy children? God was not ignorant of Lee's situation. He was moving the pieces together for an answer above and beyond anything Lee could imagine. However, at the time, living by faith and not by what could be seen was all Lee had.

Sadie had no resources for burial. Several years before, Dad had bought twelve plots in a new cemetery in the area. They were cheaper by the dozen. He didn't know who would need the plots when he made the purchase, but the first plot would be for Sadie. She would have been pleased to know that in death, she would be laid to rest in the family plot of those who had become like family to her in life.

Joyce had her back fused but had a long and painful hospitalization and recovery. She and Dale also had young children who needed care which she could not give for a long time. Relatives and the church family helped to fill in the empty place at home, but no one could really be an adequate substitute for a wife or mom.

God stirred hearts even of strangers to make a difference without knowing the impact of their efforts. Someplace in the mail delivery system, someone had a mystery to solve. There was a letter in a child's handwriting with a return address of only "Tim McDowell, La Crosse, Wisconsin" and addressed simply to: Mom, The Hospital, Eau Claire, Wisconsin. They had no McDowell listed in the hospital the envelope was sent to. Someone made some calls and found that a Mrs. McDowell was in another hospital in Eau Claire. So, the letter was sent there and delivered to Mom.

Totally unknown to anyone, Tim had written a note to his mom telling her about his first day of school, and about the papers sent home that needed a parent's signature. Then he wrote, "I'm giving you my $5 bill that I got for my birthday and it's not counterfeit. Please write and please get better quick. We are all praying for you. Love, Tim."

How that note and gift from a son, who so much yet needed her, touched Mom's heart and urged her on even more to work hard at therapy and recovery! Her face and nose needed reconstruction and even breathing was a challenge. How do you cry and wipe the tears and your nose while healing from such wounds?

When Mom finally came home from the hospital, she had a cute little pug nose, a nasal sound to her voice, and she walked with the help of crutches. The house still had only one bathroom and that was upstairs. The front living room was rearranged to improvise for all her needs until she could handle the long flight. Though her appearance and her voice had changed, the heart and soul of this wife and mother was the same. There was still a long road ahead for recovery but life was beginning to feel right again in the McDowell household now that Mom was home.

CHAPTER 13

RETREADING

The crisp fall breezes brushed their faces as Mom and Dad climbed the hill of the apple orchard. This had been a favorite family activity in the past…picking up the drops as they were called or in other orchards picking directly from the trees. These trips to the orchard were fun, but resulted in lots of work afterward.

The good apples which Mom called "keepers" could be stored in the cellar. Some would be peeled and sliced for freezing in recycled waxed milk cartons—to show up later in pies or apple crisp. The rest would be cooked for applesauce, filling the house with the aroma of apple with a hint of cinnamon. Canning was always a hot job. Besides cooking the applesauce, jars would be sterilized and filled. Next sterilized metal lids would be carefully placed on the jar. Then metal rims would be screwed tightly onto the hot jars. Finally, there was all the clean-up to do while listening for the popping sound of jars sealing. Only then was the job finished.

But this day would be different. Dad had recently retired from the railroad. Apples were ready to be harvested so pickers were hired to work the orchards. This was a fun activity Mom and Dad could enjoy together and even get paid for the bushels they picked. This time all the apples would be left at the site to be packed and sold by the orchard and Mom and Dad would come home with a small paycheck for having a day of what they considered as fun.

Dad seemed to enjoy his work whether it was on the railroad or in the orchard. In the earlier years at the freight house dock he unloaded orders shipped by rail to be delivered by truck or loaded onto another boxcar heading to another destination.

During those days, working on a railroad job was more casual than what it has become in recent years. A visit to the freight loading dock to see Dad did not have to wait for a "take your child to work" day. As Fritz's young children, we were welcomed by the work crew when we dropped in. Harry, one of Dad's coworkers, had a gift for throwing his voice. We would hear someone calling our names from across the street, but we could never see anyone. He and several of the work crew would take a little break from their lifting and loading crates, and laugh while watching us kids react to bewildering conversations with a voice that seemed to know a lot about us.

While working together, the crew developed friendships and created stories of some of their jokes and tricks on each other. Harry seemed to be behind many of the pranks on the other workers. One story that could never be retold without laughing, involved a rare time when Harry became the object of one prank. In those early times on that job, the men wore overalls with deep pockets. Someone secretly dropped something into Harry's overall pocket and waited. Harry finally reached into his deep pocket. For the longest time he fingered whatever it was that had such a strange soft yet firm texture. Finally, he pulled it out to see…and promptly threw…a dead mouse! Harry was always teasing the other guys but this time they got him.

Later Dad worked on the other side of town in the ticket office for the passenger trains. Generally he was the only one working there except during the changing of the shifts. Unlike most train depots, this one was centered in an upper-class residential part of town at the base of Granddad Bluff. It was a beautiful building with what looked like marble walls, and covering one wall was a mural of the Zephyr winding on the tracks through a typical mountain scene in the West.

Passengers and cabbies came of course, but there were times when Dad had other visitors. Sometimes a man in a drunken stupor stumbled into the depot to sleep it off. Especially when no passenger trains were due to come in and there were no passengers waiting, Dad, with a watchful eye, would let him stay if sleep and a warm place was all the man needed.

The depot was not far from the church and the parsonage. When Dad worked the night shift, Pastor Anderson would sometimes stop in during quiet times between trains. Dad was on the church board so he and Pastor shared not only a friendship but concerns related to the church and this was often an opportunity to talk over church matters.

On the railroad, a person with more seniority could bump an employee with less seniority out of a position. When Dad was bumped he went next to the freight office which was adjacent to the loading platform where he had worked with Harry and that old crew. This, though, was a desk job with the responsibility of arranging for and routing appropriate freight cars for pick-up and deliveries for companies across the country. He retired from that office after 36 years of working on the railroad.

Next was the fun job in the orchard where he and Mom could be together. They were still fairly new pickers in the orchard when life took another turn. Years earlier Mom's dad had passed away and my maternal grandma could not keep up their home. Though she had seven married children, she chose the option of moving to La Crosse to be close to Mom and Dad.

They moved Grandma into their original home on Market Street. The neighbor who had been such a challenge before the move to Dresbach had long since passed away. Grandma could live independently but still have help close by if needed.

This arrangement worked well for many years. Then when her health took an unexpected decline, Mom and Dad cleared out the front room where Mom had stayed when she was recovering from the accident, and set the room up again as a bedroom, this time for Grandma. They were no strangers to sacrificing their plans in order to meet the needs of someone else. They turned in their apple-picking ladders and bags to become caregivers for Grandma for the last six months of her life.

Grandma loved to quilt so her quilting frame was set up to be conveniently close to her. Dad kept Grandma's supply of quilting needles threaded. He even learned to quilt. Grandma took much pleasure having both Mom and Dad take turns in the chair beside the quilting frame while they would talk and sew.

Dad had been brought up under the motto that "whatever your hand finds to do, do it with all your might" …and "do it right." Though quilting and caregiving was not on Dad's "what I want to do when I retire" list, he was okay about picking up a quilting needle or a bedpan. He would do what needed to be done and do it without complaining. Even this work was done with a cheerful spirit. Mom said that sometimes she would get frustrated, but Dad was always patient.

Tim still lived at home during this time. Though he did not

participate in Grandma's care, he was respectful and considerate of her. A teenager at the time, he was trying to put pieces of the "Who am I and what am I here for?" puzzle together for himself. About this time too, Mom and Dad were taking in college students. They had extra bedrooms and there were young people who enjoyed their company and the tidbits of wisdom they shared sporadically. They were also unofficial in-house counselors and matchmakers when college kids sought advice about their love life, or relationships, or about the direction God was leading them.

By this time Jim had married Sheryl, his high school sweetheart, and he had become a police officer in La Crosse. He often could stop in on his breaks and have milk and a cookie, or a piece of pie with Mom, Dad, and Grandma.

After Grandma passed away, the idea of being a crossing guard for the schools came up. Dad, like all the McDowells, had always enjoyed children. Often stories of the antics or cute expressions of the children in their lives were the topics of entertaining conversation when the McDowells got together. One of Officer Jim McDowell's assignments at that time was overseeing the Community Services division of the police department. The school crossing guard program was one of several of those services provided through the police department. Dad responded when the city needed to hire for the upcoming school year. Getting that job meant that Jim became Dad's boss. Humbling to have your son over you? No. Dad was very proud of Jim and the position he had as a protector for the community. This only increased the bond between father and son.

Students got to know their crossing guard at his assigned elementary school as Dad loved to interact with them. He was sensitive to their need for an extra dose of attention or affirmation. One comment he teased the kids with after a fresh snowfall was "You left something behind you." They would turn to search and finding nothing would question him. "Aren't those your tracks in the snow?" he'd ask. They'd smile and move on, a little more ready to start their school day.

A yearly tradition at the school was the Teacher of the Year award. The children voted for the teacher they wished to honor and on a special assembly day each spring the children quietly waited, each hoping their choice would be the winner. One year the children and even the staff cheered when the principal announced, "And our Teacher of the Year is Fritz McDowell, our crossing guard." Actually, Dad really had been a teacher because he taught several children to tie their shoelaces while they waited to cross the street.

The day came for Dad to turn in his red stop sign, hang up his orange crossing guard vest, and retire again. By now the four older kids had married and Tim had moved out. Mom and Dad were free to go where they were needed again, to do whatever their hands found to do. And God did have new assignments for them.

People knew Dad and Mom would pray for needs they would share. Some answers to those prayers were not necessarily the way Mom and Dad would have chosen to have God answer. But, most of the time, and in time, God's wisdom in His answers could be seen.

One answer to a prayer for Terry and me came in the unexpected news that we would be moving to the other side of the world it seemed. Terry accepted a job offer in Arizona. Though four of us kids had gotten married and left home, we had always been within a few hours of La Crosse until this move.

The professional packers had already left with all the household goods, and Mom and Dad came to help with the last minute packing. Dad could visualize how to make everything else fit perfectly into every nook and cranny available in the two cars we would be driving. Saying good-bye through tears and last-minute hugs made Arizona seem really far away. The last few words were a comforting promise that Dad and Mom would make a trip to Arizona. Arm in arm the group of seven— Mom, Dad, Terry, me, and our three kids—made a circle beside the cars. Dad and Mom prayed, committing our family to the Lord's care for the long trip and our new life in Arizona. As we started the cars we looked back to see Dad put his arm around Mom. With tears blurring our eyes, we watched them, arm in arm, until our car turned the corner blocking the view between us.

Dad had always wanted to travel the country and now Mom was motivated too. Tim had been on a singing group tour and would have a concert in Phoenix the following spring. So, nine months after our move, with the last hints of winter behind them and the truck-camper packed, they drove south and then west. The plan was to see Tim in concert and to stay for about two weeks with our family. That was the beginning of yearly pilgrimages to the Southwest.

Each year they traveled to Arizona they stayed a little longer. To make life a little easier they traded the truck and camper for an RV. Mary Ann and Gil and their boys moved to California to pastor a church there. Tim settled in the West too. Now Dad and Mom had more than one reason to be on the road.

They sold their big house on Market Street and went full-time in the RV—wintering in Arizona and California, and summering in Minnesota and Wisconsin. They made new friends and learned new games in the campgrounds along the way. But was life all fun and games? In a way, yes, because they had both learned that there is joy in serving, in working at whatever job assignment God had brought them to.

Summers in Wisconsin were mostly spent at Arrowhead Bible

Camp where Mom took on the role of camp cook or sometimes kitchen helper. And Dad never lacked for things to do since he had an eye for what needed to be done no matter where he was. He had experienced so many different jobs through his life that he could fill in for many tasks.

One day one of Mom's sisters wrote her a letter saying, "I'm going to have surgery. I don't know what I am going to do with my husband [who needed care] while I am laid up." Yes, they would pray for an answer to her need and God whispered, "How about you helping?" Mom and Dad responded, pulled their RV into the farmyard, and became caregivers until her sister recovered. They did the same when Mom's brother needed the same kind of help.

Gil and Mary Ann had just relocated from California back to Minnesota when Gil suffered a stroke. Mom and Dad came to Mary Ann's rescue. They unpacked moving boxes, kept meals prepared, and did all the other practical things Mary Ann needed help with. Dad did a lot of the detailed and time-consuming investigating and paperwork related to insurance and medical bills. They offered moral support too as the family adjusted to lifestyle changes.

They parked their RV nearby or in the driveways of various grandchildren when they needed extra help with new babies, or building projects, and a host of other reasons. Whenever their RV pulled away from extended stays with the various families or from the camp, Dad left evidences that he had been there. Garages were cleaner and more organized after his visits. Every family benefited from their presence, their gentle wisdom, and their help with whatever the project was that they had worked on.

After nine years of being full-time RVers they retired to a little apartment in La Crosse. Again they were in one place long enough to be active in their home church. On Sundays if anyone wanted prayer, they could go forward to one of several people in the front who would pray for or with them. Mom and Dad often had a line of people wanting to pray with them. Approachable and genuinely caring about people and their needs, they could empathize or sympathize. Life experiences and time had prepared them for this ministry.

Many people had confided in them through the years and they had much wisdom in counseling people and praying for them. Growing up, there were many people who came into our home in Dresbach and on Market Street, often visitors sharing their needs. If we as children happened to overhear a conversation or observe someone crying or something, we were taught, "If you are not part of the problem or part of the solution, it is not to be a part of your conversation."

During those five years back in La Crosse they saw the church grow. The church purchased land for the new location in an area further from Mom and Dad's apartment. They wanted to live close to their church. Is eighty-six years old too late to start again? Not for Dad when the Lord said "Move." So, instead of signing a lease for another year in their apartment, they put their name on a contract to purchase a house near the new location of the church which by now had changed its name to First Free Church.

While the church's foundation was being poured and the walls began to take shape, Dad worked alongside his crew in the basement of their new duplex, dividing the basement into rooms, installing bathroom fixtures, and laying carpet.

Even while living in their RV during those nine years they entertained guests, sometimes for a couple weeks at a time. Now they would be prepared to open up their home to once again entertain even more guests. Home for them was always to be a place for serving people and the Lord. Even at ages eighty-six and eighty-one this would not change. Retired? "No," Dad would say. "We are retreaded." God still had work for them to do.

Dad at 86 and Mom at 81, moved in and ready to welcome more visitors to their new home.

CHAPTER 14

A GOLDEN CELEBRATION

"We need to have an open house to honor them."

"We want time to be alone just as a family."

"We should send them away for a honeymoon they did not get fifty years ago."

"We want to give them a...." and the list of ideas of what each of us wanted for our mom and dad's fiftieth anniversary to be special went on and on. Finally, ideas from the five of us siblings scattered across the country were sorted and prioritized. A plan formed but feet on the ground in La Crosse had to activate the plan and of the five children, only Jim and Sheryl lived there.

What a difference it was to plan this event compared to the wedding fifty years ago. The McDowell family had for the most part been in mourning that Fritz would be leaving the family to get married. But now, fifty years later, it was the McDowell family who volunteered eagerly to come alongside Jim and Sheryl to implement many of the details to make this day special.

Just as Elsie had stepped up to make a corsage for Mom fifty years earlier, she again would make sure there would be a corsage for Mom and a boutonniere for Dad. So typical of her to not step in boldly, she would offer suggestions hesitantly saying, "Well, do you think you might want...?" Conversations would sound very similar to this coming from her.

Dad's siblings pooled their talents to surprise Mom and Dad with a quilt of screen prints of their wedding picture plus screen prints of us five kids and our families. What had been feared so long ago that Dad's marriage would divide the family had become instead a blessing for expanding the family. Sisters-in-law and brothers-in-law had truly become a part of the close McDowell clan.

Helium balloons, bouncing in the breeze over stubborn piles of what remained of the winter snow, directed guests to the correct location. As they arrived, their presence brought a flood of wonderful memories. Faces had matured and some had wrinkled over the years but these people, these friendships, were the kind of treasures that Mom and Dad counted as precious. Even to me, just when I thought my heart was as full of joy as it could be, another guest would arrive—expanding my heart to even another level of joy. An appointment with a professional photographer brought the event to a close. No one really wanted the time for visiting to end. (Perhaps this is what heaven will be like when we reunite with loved ones who have gone on before us.)

A parade of family cars escorted Mom and Dad to their second honeymoon motel, but this honeymoon clearly was not designed for two. It would be a whole family affair. Their grandchildren who did not see each other often due to distance reconnected while decorating their grandparents' room, short-sheeting their bed and, of course, for memory's sake they hid dried beans in their grandparents' bed.

The four girl cousins spent the night in one room bonding as teens or young adults. The age difference was less noticeable than the last time they had all been together. The closeness and understanding that grew out of the weekend would carry on into their adulthood. There was a bigger age difference with the grandsons. However, the pool provided an acceptable outlet for the pent-up energies of the younger ones while the oldest grandson relaxed with his wife and two-year-old after their long drive from Arizona.

Sunday morning Mom and Dad's room was transformed into a sanctuary for a family church service. With teens propped on pillows and kids on the floor, Mom and Dad spoke freely to their offspring about events in their own lives and how the Lord brought them through challenges. They shared words of encouragement to their growing family to love the Lord and live for Him. That was the start of most of the grandchildren asking questions about family history and general advice.

For Sunday dinner, the original family of seven piled into Dad's van to go to a nice restaurant. That was the first time in twenty-five years (when I got married) that our family, just the seven of us, had been alone together. Once the door was shut, it was like stepping back in time and it was good.

What was memorable was not the fancy menu, but the sense of being united like we were as children and Dad talking to us. We felt like he was giving last instructions to his children. He shared his remorse for his failures as a father. What failures? We hadn't noticed any or at least nothing came to mind in that moment. Well, Jim finally said jokingly, "Maybe Dad meant he had given me too many spankings." We all laughed.

We joked for a while, then, in a more serious tone, Dad told us how much he appreciated each of us. He turned the conversation to things

113

he wanted us to be prepared for when something would happen to him or Mom. "Dad," I said, "you make it sound like you and Mom are getting old."

The fun and the heart-to-heart sharing was so very special. The seven of us felt a close bond. Perhaps it was the subject Dad had referred to. Perhaps it was that we sensed true enjoyment in each other's company. We all left that day craving more times of togetherness like this had been. Could such a time ever happen again?

CHAPTER 15

THE TIME MACHINE

Dad's eightieth birthday challenged the five of us kids. We so wanted to honor him, but how? He had always had a spirit of contentment with the worldly goods God had provided. His response had been the same throughout the years when asked what he wanted for a birthday or Christmas gift. "Why, I've got everything I need. All I want is for you to be good kids." A request like that was sometimes harder to grant than a request for a new shirt or some gadget would have been.

One idea surfaced with a lot of "what if's" and "could we make it work" questions. Calendars were consulted. After a few phone calls and emails, we carved out a date to reserve for celebrating.

Mom and Dad were full-time RVers, rotating between the homes of us five kids. They would be in Arizona during the appointed date. Flights were arranged. Mary Ann would leave Gil for the first time since his stroke. Janice would fly in just after her college-age son had gone through his cancer surgery. Tim had recently moved out of an abusive roommate situation and was learning to live in a little safer living arrangement. Terry had just become unemployed again. And just before his day to fly to Arizona, Jim's mother-in-law had a serious health crisis. Each one was living on our own edge of personal trials.

Grandson Rick and his wife had just moved into a new house within twenty miles of Terry's and my house. The original intent was for the five kids and Mom and Dad to have a few days together at a motel. But Rick insisted that he, his wife, and their four-year-old Heidee would move in with his wife's folks for the weekend, and we could use their house. All seven (Mom, Dad, Stella, Mary Ann, Janice, Jim, and Tim) would be together for one week-end under one roof—just like it was so many years ago.

With each trip to the airport excitement and laughter increased and so did the number of passengers in the van. It was time to forget personal crises and focus instead on honoring Dad. The childhood wish for time with just our family that had been so treasured was about to become a reality for a whole weekend. It was like stepping back in time with the fun and frolicking of a child but with the additional benefit of an adult perspective.

Some flights were delayed and some passengers' flight plans changed en route. Thus it happened that each one arrived in the order of their birth. That meant Tim was the last to arrive.

We all waited at the gate. This was before the airlines changed their policy about where travelers could connect with those waiting for them. The PA system announced that the gate for the plane Tim was arriving on had been changed. No surprise. Flight plans for each traveler had been changed often through the day. We hustled through the terminal to the newly assigned gate.

Our plan was to duplicate some special events that had been a part of our lives together years ago. This time, instead of peeking through an open door on the maternity floor of the hospital as we had done to get our first glimpse of our baby brother, Dad, Mom, and all four of us older siblings lined up at the airline gate with "It's a boy" balloons and a banner that read "The Party Starts Here". We brought noisemakers, but they proved useless for announcing his arrival as we were laughing so much we couldn't pucker our lips around the horn. Tim rolled his sparkling eyes when he walked through the gateway door and saw us with the balloons and the sign. He tried in vain to pretend that all this attention was not for him.

Now our family was complete. All of us, except maybe Tim, walked through the airport oblivious to onlookers. Laughing and hugging, and carrying our sign and balloons, we jostled our way to the baggage carousel to gather the last of the luggage we would be hauling home from the airport for the weekend. We were ready to celebrate.

The emotional load each was carrying would be shared but for now that was set aside. We relished the joy and sense of safety and comfort we felt in coming together as a family. Unknown to us during that ride from the airport to the house was how much we would be getting acquainted with one another as adults. Other than our restaurant dinner together three years earlier, the times we had been together were occupied with juggling kids and meal preparations.

The van pulled up to my house. Terry, Pam, our daughter, and our oldest son Rick and his family welcomed the familiar travelers and joined in with the joking and laughing. The twelve of us held hands as we bowed our heads for a genuine prayer of gratitude for food and family. Contagious laughter peppered our conversation and the comical stories of each traveler's airport adventures. Heidee looked from one adult to another, not understanding what was so funny but still giggling right along with the adults.

Rick had a gift for his grandpa to open before the seven would head over to his house. Dad laughed when he saw the contraption. It was a pie tin with slots and a belt woven through the slots. Rick had written up a poem, too, about this stump riding saddle. Most of us were still clueless so Dad told his story that he had already relayed to Rick.

"Barry (Dad's brother-in-law) and I had cut down an old pear tree at De Soto. We left about a four-foot stump so we could heave it back and forth to loosen the root. We had been pushing and pulling on it for some time before the root suddenly gave way. Barry had been doing the pulling and he fell to the ground on his back. When he went down, I went flying up onto the top of the stump. Barry had his breath knocked out of him and I was stuck up in the air with my stomach centered on the crosscut of the stump. I couldn't do anything. Neither my hands nor my feet could touch the ground. Barry was knocked out and I was stuck. Jessie saw our predicament from the house and came on the run. By the time she got to us, Barry had caught his breath and together they were able to free me from my perch."

Dad finished his story but the rest of us were belly laughing so hard our sides hurt. We had to pass the tissue box around because some of us laughed so hard we cried. We regained our composure and Rick slipped his new house key onto Dad's key ring. Dad and Mom and their five grown-up "little ones" headed the van toward their home for the weekend and what Dad would call later "our little bit of heaven on earth." Though we had been together in the restaurant for a couple hours for their 50th anniversary, this would be the first time in over thirty-five years we would be living together, at least for a week-end, under one roof. Just the seven of us and it was very good.

Like kids moving into a new house, we each put in a claim for the room we thought fit us best. Mom and Dad had their own beds in their RV parked alongside Rick's house. The three of us girls claimed the master bedroom with the master bathroom. Tim chose the guest room with the king-sized bed and Jim, who was much bigger than Tim, took what was left—the small twin size bed in Heidee's room. With suitcases in their proper rooms we settled down to the business at hand...honoring Dad for his eightieth birthday.

With much drumroll and fanfare Mary Ann pinned Dad with an "Aged to Perfection" merit badge to be worn throughout our weekend. Then in keeping with our theme that Dad was to be king of the hill (since we used to live on a hill), we presented him with an antigravity lounge chair as his throne, and of course his queen needed a throne too so both Dad and Mom unwrapped their look-alike gifts.

Jim had written a poem about Dad being king of the road (in his RV) and we sang the poem to the tune of the sixties Roger Miller song, "King of the Road." Jim's story line poem was humorous and accurate with Dad and family history in mind. We shared some of the memories of how Dad's faith and trust in the Lord were fleshed out in his actions and how that affected us.

Nobody wanted the evening to end until Dad repeated an old line he had often used, "Say, it's getting late. You kids better get to bed." We were ready to comply. We prayed together before heading to our bedrooms. It had been a long but very good day and there was more to come.

Mary Ann and I woke up first and whispered much like old times though the whispered subjects had changed over the years. When we heard Janice stirring from her floor mattress bed, we said, "Come up here," and she joined us in bed. Our sisters-only conversation stalled when we heard Jim was awake. We got up, grabbed our bathrobes, and went to check. Once both Jim and Tim were up, we reminisced about how we all used to crawl in bed with Mom and Dad on Saturday mornings. Well, we wouldn't all fit now but one of us ran down to the RV and let Mom and Dad know that we were all awake and to come upstairs for a surprise.

By the time they got to the top of the stairs the five of us were in the king-sized bed with bathrobes over our PJs. Five adults hardly fit. But they laughed at the sight of their five not so little cherubs all lined up in bed. Of course they had to get a picture. We were REALLY hot by the time they grabbed a camera. As soon as they snapped the picture, we bolted to get dressed in something cool and start our day of adventures.

Going to the apple orchard as a family wasn't really a tradition. It was just something we did every fall. Our part of Arizona cannot boast of having apple orchards but there are lots of citrus trees. I had made arrangements to pick the grapefruit for an elderly lady who really could use help stripping her trees. There would be plenty of fruit for the Wisconsin and Minnesota siblings to take back with them.

Dad was not a swimmer but he used to hand toss us into the Mississippi River. We never got enough of those tosses into the waves at the beach. So, in reviving a bit of that history and because the northerners wanted to swim while they were in Arizona, Dad pointed the van to a fitness center for some walk-aerobics and a swim.

Dad stood in chest deep water while we exercised by treading water around him between swimming laps. He told the story again of why he never learned to swim. His uncle had drowned in the river and because of that his mother had not wanted her kids near the river. "Living close to the river, I wanted you kids to know how to swim," he said. "I wanted you kids to have skills I never possessed." We knew he wanted us to be prepared as much as possible for whatever rivers or challenges in life we might encounter.

We did one thing we had never ever done before. Tim had not yet been born when we had a family train trip to Montana. By the time Dad took the family on the next traveling vacation, I was married. So, for the first time ever, for his eightieth birthday Dad took his whole family on a vacation. He maneuvered the RV out of the driveway and beaming, he drove his big rig with his family seated beside or behind him. We were heading to the mountains for our first whole family getaway. Though it was only a thirty-five to forty-mile trip, we played our roles well. Echoes of "We're hungry" and "How many more miles?" and "Are we almost there?" came from the back of the RV.

We took a short walk at the mountain lake, ate our picnic lunch along with bees that joined us (an unexpected memory of Ben's bees in Dresbach), and after two or three hours we packed up for our trip home. Dad treated us to ice cream in honor of repeating memories of treats from years past.

Jim had brought his video camera but cameras seemed to get in the way and for the most part were laid aside. We were all too involved in just living in the present moment rather than thinking of preserving the memories we were remaking during that weekend. We did, however, get a professional photograph taken. As we waited for the photographer, we considered the best parts of each one to show off for the camera: Mary Ann's polished nails, Tim's mustache, my gray hair. It was all a part of being silly and amounted to almost none of those good points showing up in the picture.

We ate simply—simply the best meals ever—including family favorites like creamed eggs on toast and scalloped potatoes with ham. Whatever else we had did not require a recipe. It was Mom's cooking, plus a few other hands in the pot, hands that had learned to cook at her side. We just knew from experience how to cook well, eat well, and do

123

so frugally. Mom had taught us.

This weekend the original family was reconnecting on an adult level. As we played and worked together, we shared on a deeper level than we had time to do in a very long time. We had drifted away from each other, not intentionally, but we each had become entrenched in our own responsibilities and our own families. Naturally those families had become the ones who were at the forefront of our time and attention.

Evenings were the best. We played Dirty Marbles, Hand and Foot, and Rook and munched on Mom's caramel corn. We shared what was going on currently in our lives and we shared our memories. So often when we would say something about how we remembered something, we asked questions like, "What was really happening when….?" As kids, we had seen or experienced things from a child's point of view. Now Mom and Dad shared those same things we had brought up in ways which now, as adults we could appreciate, sometimes revealing why they made the choices they did. Dad and Mom explained some things we would not have understood as children. Even then, because many people came to them with problems, they still were true to keeping confidences. As children, we may have observed someone crying or sharing a conversation with Mom or Dad but we had been taught that if we were not part of a problem or part of a solution, that subject was not to be a part of our conversations. That conviction did not change with the passing of time.

One misunderstanding none of us had realized was clarified involving Tim, the youngest, and me, the oldest by sixteen years. I shared that the memories everyone else was recalling from the second Market Street house was not much of a part of my history. I was married almost three years after we moved into that house so I did not live there very long. It seemed that sharing this made a light bulb go off in Tim's mind.

He could also identify with that. He said that he always felt that he had missed out because we so often talked of our lives in Dresbach and he was not born until after we moved from there.

Now the obvious dawned. Though we all were in the same family, the places and events that shaped our lives were not the same for each of us. This realization seemed to dissolve feelings of being left out and opened doors of better understanding.

Evenings were also a time for talking naturally of the challenges, crises, and joys each of us was going through. Though Tim was not walking with the Lord during this time and though he did not pray verbally, he was still a part of this sharing and caring that took place. Hearing Dad pray for each of us, naming us and presenting our specific needs and concerns to the Lord, was precious beyond words. We all knew Mom and Dad prayed for us. It had been their practice to pray audibly together before they would go to sleep. Even the adult grandchildren told stories of standing outside their closed bedroom door and listening to their muffled voices as they prayed.

Sunday morning our family routine had been to go to church and while we were young kids we sat together as a family during the service. We did the same this day but we took up a much larger portion of a pew this time. The pastor of our church announced that Dad was having a special birthday celebration and that his whole family was with him today. Dad stood at the pastor's invitation and spoke. His voice quivered, "It's been like a little bit of heaven to have this weekend together."

After church we shared our Sunday dinner and conversation around a table. Then as we gathered in a circle before separating to head to the airport and Dad thanked the Lord for our family and for the blessing of being together for this weekend. Laughs and tears mingled with hugs as Tim, Jim, Janice, and Mary Ann boarded their fights. Each one renewed, refreshed, and ready or not, was headed back to our adult lives with all the challenges awaiting us. The prayers, renewed memories, and deepened relationships we had experienced during the weekend had been a respite for each of us. Words and maybe reason fail to explain how it worked but during those few days together we all had seemed to fit into the same roles we had as children.

Though we had demonstrated honor and appreciation to Dad and Mom, we were the ones who were blessed in the process. In keeping with the request he always made when asked about what he'd want for gifts, it seemed that Dad felt he had really received what he wanted most for his eightieth birthday.

Celebrating Dad's 80th birthday

Left to right: Jim, Mom, Janice, Tim, Dad, Mary Ann, and Stella

CHAPTER 16

THIS IS YOUR LIFE

The eightieth birthday had been a highlight for every one of the seven family members. By the time Dad was to celebrate his ninetieth birthday everyone wanted more of the same kind of experience we had shared ten years earlier but this time spouses would participate at least for some of the weekend. By this time Mom and Dad had given up roaming in the RV and had become homeowners again so we all went home to them for a weekend.

Though spouses had joined for this celebration we still wanted a large portion of Saturday for just our original family. After breakfast together just Dad, Mom, and the five of us kids loaded into the van. Jim took the role of tour guide/driver with Dad riding beside him.

Particularly since their fiftieth anniversary the family had done a lot of asking questions and striving to pick Dad and Mom's brain about how they had made life work and what had gone into the development of their marriage and their walk with the Lord. Today would be no different.

It was a short ride to Riverside Park where Jim parked the van. Mom and Dad's eyes still sparkled as they retold the story of how they met and of the time they were parked in this very spot. Mom had shared with her boyfriend that day how Jesus had paid the price for our sin. We were in the very place where Dad's relationship with the Lord began.

The next stop was at the address of the first place they had lived as newlyweds. The building was long gone but the address was correct. While parked there, they retold the story of the gaps between the floorboards and of Mom and her bee sting. Being in that setting prompted more questions of what living conditions were like there in the early forties.

Jim turned the van to Market Street. We parked briefly in front of the two houses where the memories began at one house for the older children and the second house where memories began for Tim. Shared stories of experiences of living in these houses stimulated more questions and memories.

Then Jim drove the ten miles to Dresbach. That beloved home where so much life had happened had been destroyed to make room for the freeway. The face of the hills had been blasted or bulldozed away. Some of our neighbors' houses had been moved back from their original foundation to meet the requirements specified by the highway department. Other homes had been destroyed like ours had been. Since the highway had "redesigned" even the hills, it was hard to determine the exact location where home had been.

Jim stopped the van in town and we all got out to hunt for old landmarks. There had been one store in town when we lived there. One corner of the store served as the post office for the town where we would pick up mail. The store also served as the cross-country bus stop. The one gas station in town was the gathering place for junior and senior high school students to wait for the driver to start the bus that I think was housed in the garage of the station.

Since our absence, Dresbach had attracted new residents and a landscape of upscale waterfront homes. Of the remaining familiar buildings, several had been modernized. Even the beach area had been updated and enlarged. Still, our family lamented that things just were not what they had been in the "glory days" of the fifties.

An old apple orchard stand was the next stop. Very little had changed there it seemed. The scent of fall and apples remained the same. The sound of crunching into a crisp Macintosh or Cortland and the taste of the juicy apples were just as we remembered. Nature had not changed.

"Where to now, Jim?" He was driving south on highway 61, not a route commonly used in earlier years.

"De Soto," he answered, "by way of Lansing, Iowa. Doesn't everyone want to cross the bridge?" That had been a major subject of their first date story. Jim was always one to think ahead and throw in surprises. The toll bridge was gone, but there was still a bridge for crossing the Mississippi between Iowa and Wisconsin.

By going through Lansing first, we were entering De Soto from the south instead of the north. Though it was not the usual route, we knew exactly where to go. The house Dad and his family had built after the fire of 1926 had recently been sold to a shirttail relative. They invited any of the McDowell family to return anytime. They had already opened the home for the annual McDowell family event, Aunts Day.

The new owners had been attracted to the house because of its "oldness" and the sense they had of it being a child-friendly home. They went to great effort to maintain the "antique" (strange word to use of something so familiar to us) appearance of the house even in their process of updating things like fixtures and appliances. They had chosen a claw-foot bathtub and a new kitchen stove reflecting the appearance of antique ones that once were showcased in old Sears catalogs.

The new owners welcomed us just as they had said they would. They basically stood aside and invited us to wander through the house and reminisce. They even asked questions about how things used to be arranged in the house and a host of other questions they had thought of since moving in.

We walked the paths of the yard that had been home to Dad and had been the "down home" as it was known to all of the McDowells' offspring. We noticed the garden, smaller than it had been when it was providing for the very large McDowell family. We reminisced about things like ground cherries and homegrown popcorn. We peeked into the second-floor attic where we remembered braided popcorn shucks had always been stored with the kernels exposed for the drying process. As children, when we had overnights with our grandparents and Aunts Alberta and Jessie, who also lived there, we often made trips to the attic to rub off enough dry kernels to pop for our bedtime treats. The larger kernels nearest the base of the cobs dried first and released from the cob more easily. They were rough, even sharp it seemed, and poked our hands as we freed them from the cob.

The mulberry tree where we plucked snacks when the berries were ripe was long gone. We peered over the embankment into the lower wooded area where Aunts Alberta and Jessie sometimes took us out into the woods to look for wildflowers in the spring. They also knew where we could go beyond the road to gather hickory nuts in the fall if squirrels or other nut hunters had not already collected the harvest. That spurred memories of the stained fingers from the walnut husks before the walnuts were dried. There had always been a pile of nut shells by the anvil in the toolshed where one could help himself anytime to nuts,

132

provided he was willing to crack them and dig out the nutmeats.

We reminisced about digging for worms with Aunt Etta. She would find cane fishing poles for each of us and lead a troop of cousins carrying our poles down the hill to the river's edge. We rarely caught anything worth keeping, but when the bobs dipped indicating some action on our lines, we got excited. Etta would chuckle while telling us to be quiet so we wouldn't scare the fish away. If we actually pulled our lines up with a little sunfish or perch, it was a time of rejoicing. If we happened to get a bullhead on our line, then there was not so much to cheer about. Etta had to put on a heavy glove and handle the bullhead with care while digging the hook out of its mouth.

My siblings recalled being lined up on the kitchen floor with the cousins about their age waiting while our aunts scooped ice cream into cones for each of them. We remembered the old dining room table extended as far as the extra table leaves allowed with flannel pieces and pajama patterns spread out on top.

Between Thanksgiving and Christmas, the aunts made gifts for their twenty-nine nieces and nephews. On years they made pajamas, we often became short-term mannequins when they came up with pattern deviations for a cousin "about your size" they claimed. Other years they knitted mittens for us. That would have been fifty-eight mittens if we all got a pair.

For Easter, all the cousins who were lucky enough to get "down home" (meaning De Soto) helped color eggs with our aunts. Aunt Elsie always led that activity. Easter at De Soto meant lots of eggs in lots of hiding places with lots of cousins scampering around the huge yard. Whenever Elsie was involved with anything, it would be extra fun. She even had us cousins convinced that her favorite game was Candy Land. She tried to tell us that if she stayed busy with us, she would get out of doing dishes. We laughed that off because we knew she just liked to play with us.

We created our own Aunts Day many years before someone, likely Hallmark, officially proclaimed one in 2008. Ours was an extra time for the extended family to demonstrate appreciation back to each of our five single aunts. Etta, Jessie, Jenny, Alberta, and Elsie poured expressions of "I love you," "you're important," and "I really like being with you" into each of the twenty-nine of us. We had kind of a mutual admiration society with our aunts. If persistent love and forgiveness had not been a part of our family's past, how different our memories may have been.

Left to right: Jessie, Jenny Alberta, Etta, and Elsie.

With a sigh the seven of us piled back into the van with freshly recalled history and some new insights into our past. It had been a good day.

By the time we pulled into the driveway of what was now home to Mom and Dad, the casserole Mom had prepared for Sheryl, to put in the oven was hot. The sons-in-law and a handyman friend had spent the day installing a screen door as a surprise. Dad would not have asked for this. He never asked for a tangible gift. He said again, and maybe this time it was because even this was a part of family tradition, "The best gift you could give me is for you to be good kids."

Sunday afternoon we hosted an Open House at Jim and Sheryl's house. Among the guests was one of the girls who had lived with Mom and Dad during a portion of her college days. She had a very personal conversation with Dad which she didn't want to forget so she rushed home to record it. Now twenty years after writing it, and still a very close friend of our family, she handed that note to me saying, "You can share this if you wish." It was so typical of the kinds of conversations Dad had with people. None would have been the same as he spoke to each person's particular situation and need. This in part is what Cathy Smith handed to me.

November 5, 2006, Fritz's 90th Birthday Celebration. As I was getting ready to leave, this is what was said:

"This was a great day for you, Fritz."

"Yes, it was and I had six kids here."

It didn't register with me so he said it again. Then he explained that I was the sixth one. He made me cry as he held my hand and looked into my teary eyes.

This was my family talk from the mentor of all times. I hugged him a second time. He began to tell me how much I have meant to him and Mae.

I said how that feeling is mutual and how I cherished their prayers for all these years.

He said how they also appreciated my prayers for them so we are just taking care of one another.

I mentioned what an impact their lives have been on me and so many others.

He responded, "People say that and give us credit but we haven't done anything out of the ordinary." He proceeded to say that how I handled difficult situations showed a lot about my commitment. I said I made a choice and needed to live by it.

He also said I spoke my mind on things when it wasn't easy… (more tears).

"Tears aren't all bad. They show our heart," Fritz said as he proceeded to hold my hand to let me know he wasn't done…. I think what made me cry more was the sense

of Fritz being the patriarch of his physical and spiritual family and I was included in a dear part of his and Mae's heart.

I was overcome thinking that he was taking care of his

final business with each one there over the weekend…giving his blessing on their lives and on mine. The conversation continued until someone else came over to say good-bye."

~

None of us—not even this friend who thought Fritz was giving people a final blessing—could have imagined that this was to be the last time all seven of us would be together.

Open house for Dad's 90th birthday.

Back row: Jim and Tim.

Front row: Janice, Stella, Dad, Mom, and Mary Ann

CHAPTER 17

THE HOMECOMING

What was admittedly the heaviest burden Dad and Mom had to deal with cannot be omitted from this story. They had been praying for almost thirty years one consistent prayer, trusting God would answer, not knowing if they would live to see it or not.

The Child Evangelism teacher who had come for a special meeting with children stayed at Mom and Dad's house. Five-year-old Tim attended the meeting which ended with an invitation for the children to raise their hand if they wanted Jesus to be their Savior. After they had all come home from the meeting, Tim tugged on the arm of the teacher. "I raised my hand too."

"I'm sorry. I didn't see you, Tim. Why did you raise your hand?"

Tim answered, "I want Jesus to come into my heart." Together the two of them sat on the porch steps while the teacher explained the same things Mom had explained to Dad so many years ago when Dad made that same decision to receive the gift of salvation. That day Tim became a child of God through confessing that he had disobeyed God and that God's only begotten Son, Jesus, loved him enough to be the perfect

: so he could be forgiven and Tim accepted Jesus as his Savior.

Tim followed in the footsteps of his older siblings: attending Sunday school, church, and Bible camp. His musical and drama talents put him on his high school and community stages and later he toured with a Christian group giving concerts throughout much of America and Europe.

Tim and Janice were close and would talk freely with each other even when Tim confided in Janice his questioning of his sexuality. Janice remembers one conversation with Tim. He said, "My friends tell me that it's okay to have this alternative lifestyle. They say a person is born having these kinds of desires. Deep down, I know, though, it really is sin." Even that early conviction was not enough to keep him from questioning his own conscience and then distorting what he knew God's Word says.

The tactics of the Tempter starts out with the "Did God really say _____?" question. Causing doubt about what God says opens the door to think of reasons why the activity in question is all right. Then the Tempter, the deceiving Destroyer, whispers, "God made you with these desires and He wants you to be happy." The continuation of entertaining those thoughts instead of focusing on God's Word and one's relationship with the Lord wears one down until a person becomes convinced that what God said isn't valid in "my" particular case.

Dad and Mom were familiar with Tim's friends but Tim had another group of friends Dad and Mom were not aware of. Tim was deceptive about his interactions with these friends who influenced him toward decisions that led him on a downward spiral. The friends Mom and Dad were aware of supported Tim with encouragement from God's Word and with accountability regarding his Christian life. When one of those Christian friends died in an unusual accident, Tim was devastated and just sort of gave in to the sin which had such a strong downward pull on him and to the activities which once had been repulsive to him.

Tim shared his struggles with one of those good friends who encouraged Tim and continued to speak biblical truth into his life even while Tim was not receptive to what was being shared. Throughout the years though, this friend and Tim maintained a strong mutual friendship.

It was a dark day when Mom and Dad became aware that the way Tim was living and the way he wanted them to think he was living were two different things. They spent many days and nights grieving over his choices. When Tim told them that he was gay, they felt physically, mentally, emotionally, and spiritually just sick. Mom shared that her heart hurt so much it was like her chest was crushing, making even breathing difficult. Just the thought of what Tim was doing made them feel dirty and nauseous like they had never experienced before.

On the heels of the first waves of grief came the guilt. They questioned themselves, "Where did we go wrong?" And they came up with a mental list of whys that continued to feed their guilt. They concluded they were not fit to serve the Lord since they had failed with Tim.

For years their shame and pain was too deep to share with those outside our immediate family. Where could they go but to the Lord? They would not give up on this son. Tim had always referred to that time when he was five as the time he received the gift of forgiveness of sin and of salvation. How could Tim have embraced these choices for his life? They would have doubted the genuineness of that earlier decision to trust in Jesus if they had never seen what appeared to them as spiritual growth in his life. They knew salvation is not based on a person's sexual preference or anything else a person does but purely on acknowledging personal sin and believing in and trusting in Jesus, Who alone, as the sinless Son of God, was qualified and willing to pay the penalty our sin deserves. But, if a person really believes, if that really is the foundation of a person's life, it should be evidenced by actions:

> Do not be deceived: Neither the sexually immoral nor idolaters nor adulterers nor men who have sex with men nor thieves nor the greedy nor drunkards nor slanderers nor swindlers will inherit the kingdom of God. And that is what some of you were. But you were washed, you were sanctified, you were justified in the name of the Lord Jesus Christ and by the Spirit of our God...Flee from sexual immorality. All other sins a person commits are outside the body, but whoever sins sexually, sins against their own body. Do you not know that your bodies are temples of the Holy Spirit, who is in you, whom you have received from God? You are not your own; you were bought at a price. Therefore honor God with your bodies (1 Corinthians 6: 9b-11, 18–20 NIV).

Some of us wondered about Tim's eternal destiny because of his choices but God's Word also says:

> All those the Father gives me will come to me, and whoever comes to me I will never drive away. For I have come down from heaven not to do my will but to do the will of him who sent me. And this is the will of him who sent me, that I shall lose none of all those he has given me, but raise them up at the last day. For my Father's will is that everyone who looks to the Son and believes in him shall have eternal life, and I will raise them up at the last day (John 6: 37- 40 NIV).

Regardless of a person's bent to any particular sin, we are all guilty of sin. Sin is in essence telling or showing God that "I know better than You. I will live my life the way I want to no matter what You say." All sin grieves God's heart. As people, we tend to divide sins into little and big ones but any one sin makes us sinners. Some sins bring destruction to our physical bodies more than others but all sin robs us of God's intended good blessing for us when He made man. Even when we reject Him, He still loves us. "But God demonstrates his own love for us in this: While we were yet sinners, Christ died for us" (Romans 5:8 NIV).

We all are loved by God and need forgiveness from Him. We all deal with various temptations. How we respond either draws us closer to the Lord or, if we yield to the temptation, we draw away from God. We see that in the story of Adam and Eve's response when they disobeyed God in Genesis chapter 3 and then they hid from God.

Tim's yielding to temptation caused him to draw away from God and initially to draw away from the family. For a while he chose to room with friends and then he moved out of state. His response to sin was not unlike Adam and Eve's. Nevertheless, Mom and Dad continued to pray and trust God to bring their son back to the Lord, whether the answer came in their lifetime or not.

Tim identified himself with his lifestyle by saying, "But this is who I am." Each family member had to figure out for himself or herself how to continue to love Tim and yet show how God's heart (and ours) breaks over sin that will eventually hurt him. We individually had to stumble our way through that process, not always agreeing. Love is seeking the best for the other person. How to do that did not look the same to each family member. One thing we all could agree on was that we needed to pray—pray for Tim's relationship with the Lord to be restored, for wisdom to know how to relate to him, and for understanding the confusion and questions and attitudes all this forced us to struggle with. We absolutely wanted to obey God even in our humanly inadequate finite understanding of how to hate the sin and love the sinner.

For a while, Tim just making contact with the family was something to be thankful for. He was always welcome to come home and eventually he came for short visits even when his relocations took him several states away from Wisconsin. When Tim did visit, Dad and Mom made it to be as special as they could. Except for the time Mom and Dad were full time in their RV, they had a piano or keyboard waiting at home for Tim to bring those black-and-white keys to life. Mom would stop what she was doing and sit beside him while he played and sang.

Whenever the family or part of the family was together, games like Rook, Dirty Marbles, or Hand and Foot were favorites all could enjoy and share lighthearted conversation while joking with each other. Some games required teamwork strategy consultations. This was one way all of us could connect with Tim in an easy and natural way. He came from across the country to participate in events like weddings of nieces and nephews and the big anniversary and birthday celebrations for Dad and Mom. Even during those visits, Tim would often choose to slip out alone for the evening. Regardless of what he may have thought, his deceptions, self-centeredness, and manipulation tactics were not totally concealed. Eventually his health was compromised.

While Jim was counting down the months for his retirement, he was making plans for all the free time he would have. "Dad and Mom, after I retire this summer, Sheryl and I are taking you to Arizona probably in August to see Stella's family and your newest great-granddaughter." This was several years after Dad had given up driving cross-country so they had not seen my family very often. Tim planned to drive over three hundred miles from the place he lived at the time to Arizona to visit all of us the first part of September.

In the spring Tim began having some health problems and was having tests. It was July when he called Janice with the news. "The most recent test came back, Jan. It looks like I have myelodysplastic syndrome. Will you help me tell Mom and Dad?"

Jan did some research on it before she and Tim called them.

"What did you call it, Jan?" Mom and Dad had never heard of this before.

Knowing they would not understand medical details and terminology, Jan explained, "It's something like a form of leukemia."

"Oh, Tim...." For a while there were no words as they tried to take in what this meant. "What are the doctors doing for you, Tim?"

"I get blood transfusions and that helps until I get too weak and need another one." Later in the conversation he added, "The doctor is giving me only a couple years..." Again only silent sadness as three hearts—the parents and their son—were reaching out to embrace so inadequately over the phone lines. "It will be good to see you."

When they hung up the phone, Mom and Dad looked at each other in disbelief. As they had done many times before, they fell back on what they knew about God. This did not surprise Him, He is still sovereign. He loved Tim even more than they did. They wondered, "Is this how God is going to bring Tim back to the Lord?" The trip took on new urgency, but there was a sense of peace that God had prearranged this trip so Dad and Mom would be in Arizona and be able to see Tim.

Barely had Jim pulled Dad's van into our driveway at the end of August when Tim called. He did not feel well enough to drive to Arizona. He needed another transfusion. Could the four of them drive to him? Then he talked to Mom. "Mom, I'm scared..."

~

145

Our daughter, Pam, and her husband hosted the travelers plus our son and his family, and Terry and me for supper. The great-grandchildren were delightful diversions for the weary travelers, but their real focus was getting back on the road again. If Tim was scared, Mom and Dad wanted to be there for him. The next day they did their laundry and we made some favorite family treats for Tim. We all went to Rick's house for a swim and a cookout that evening, but cut the visit short so they could get back to our house and get a good night's sleep before starting out for Tim's place.

By the time they arrived at Tim's the following evening, it was pretty evident that his body was so compromised that he would succumb to this illness much sooner than the two years the doctor had initially given him. He needed transfusions more frequently than what the doctor had first expected and he gave Tim a new prognosis of only weeks to live. After receiving that news, Tim chose to return to his apartment where his medical needs would be supervised through the local hospice program. Tim's friend Alvin worked together with Jim, rearranging furniture and setting up a hospital bed in the living room for Tim. Mom, Dad, Jim, and Sheryl stayed in a nearby hotel but were with Tim much of the time.

Even with Tim being so sick, Mom laid down beside him on the hospital bed. She wrapped her arms around him like she had done with all her children when we were young. They talked about heaven and where Tim was in his relationship with the Lord. Tim's words were "Don't worry, Mom. I'm ready to go to heaven; I've made it right with God." Tim went on to tell how he had shared the gospel with his friend and led him to the Lord. Tim had taken his friend to visit some churches to find one the two of them could attend until he was too sick to continue that search.

On Tim's good days they took Tim out for rides so he could show them his world or they visited and laughed as they recounted family stories and munched on Mom's homemade caramel corn. On other days they watched sports on TV or videos of recent family activities. Tim had been anxious to see the video of a nephew's wedding in Wisconsin. There had been a blizzard and though many guests who lived much closer to the event could not get through the snow, Tim had made it all the way to Wisconsin to be the pianist for the ceremony. The wedding had only been eight months earlier and Tim had not complained of unusual symptoms at that time.

Increasingly, Tim had more days when he was too weak to do anything. Jim, with his big hands and gentle heart, moved out of his comfort zone, donned gloves, and helped Alvin care for him. Of course, the two men were not nurses, but they could do some of his daily personal care and they learned how to provide some comfort measures and deal with the catheter (which definitely was not a comfort measure in Tim's opinion). One day while the two were working together, Alvin surprised Jim by saying, "Jim, I want to be a godly man like you."

At times Jim would call one of his nurse sisters (mostly Janice, the RN) for advice on how to better care for Tim. They did have a resource hospice nurse, but could not always get in contact as quickly with her as they would have liked. Sometimes Jim just wanted to talk things over with Janice about what was happening medically.

Love showed up strongly in the actions of caring for Tim while, at the same time, we hated the choices Tim had made that had brought him to this point. Tim was told that his diagnosis was not related to his lifestyle but being HIV positive had compromised his body and contributed to his rapid decline.

In another conversation with Mom and Dad, Tim said. "I'll soon be singing in heaven with Keith Green" (one of the late Christian musicians Tim enjoyed). Then Tim asked, "Do you still have a burial plot in La Crosse for me? I want to be taken back there."

Dad and Mom had thought they would likely die before their son would turn back to the Lord, but God had a better plan. He had that trip arranged long before Tim had even gotten sick. They would be present to hear with their own ears and see with their own eyes the answer to their prayers.

His friend wanted a funeral for Tim where they lived for people they both knew. So Alvin planned one to be held at a nearby funeral home. There were flowers but no pastor, no program, and only canned background music. People who had come just mulled around quietly waiting, as if someone should be saying something. Introducing himself as he stood, Jim had their attention. He identified who Dad, Mom, and Sheryl were and then he talked about his brother. Jim also shared that Tim was now in heaven, not because of any good works Tim did, but because Tim had confessed his sin and asked Jesus to forgive him. No one can be good enough to be accepted into the presence of a holy God but God did provide a way for any of us to be acceptable to Him. He quoted John 3:16-18:

> For God so loved the world that he gave his one and only Son, that whoever believes in him shall not perish but have eternal life. For God did not send his Son into the world to condemn the world, but to save the world through him. Whoever believes in him is not condemned, but whoever does not believe stands condemned already because they have not believed in the name of God's one and only Son [NIV].

Tim's friends listened. Some came to speak with the family, some thanking Jim for his words and some sharing how they knew Tim.

Tim was brought back to Wisconsin for a second funeral where most of the family could attend. Jim, Sheryl, Mom, and Dad made record time driving to Wisconsin. My flight from Arizona got me to La Crosse before Dad, Mom, Jim, and Sheryl were due to arrive so they would not have to come home to an empty house and so that I could start making room arrangements for the out of town relatives who would be coming. When Jim and I went to order flowers for the top of the casket, Jim said Alvin had been very specific about the flowers he had chosen for the funeral he had arranged. In consideration of Alvin, we decided to order a spray of flowers as much as possible like the one he had chosen. He would be flying to La Crosse for this funeral also.

The next evening Jim went to pick him up from the airport and I was about to meet this friend of Tim's for the first time—or so I thought. Without making excuses for my attitude, I will admit that I was dreading this meeting. Alvin's plane was delayed so by the time he arrived for dinner, the evening was late. During our introductions, he mentioned that he had met me before.

"When?" I asked.

"When I picked up Tim after your daughter's wedding."

Six years earlier when my daughter was getting married, Tim had asked about bringing his new friend to the wedding and I had said "No." On the rare occasions I had met Tim's likeminded friends before, my internal stress level was raised a notch. As mother of the bride, and with the house full of extra company, I didn't feel I needed that extra stress on Pam's wedding day. I clearly was focused on other things that day as apparently I met him after the wedding without realizing who he was. The conversation around the table with the family was pleasant but there

149

was very little time after dinner before we each went to homes or motel rooms to sleep.

That night the Lord convicted me so clearly that I needed to ask forgiveness. What? Me? I struggled with that but could not shake the idea that God was asking me to do this. My "but God" excuses failed to silence His prompting. At last I surrendered. If God provided an opportune time I would obey. The next day various ones of us were in and out of Mom and Dad's house doing errands that needed to be done before the visitation that evening. Alvin and Jim were about to leave the house and knowing what I needed to do, I followed them outside. Looking at Alvin, I spoke, "I need to ask you something. I'm sorry. Will you forgive me?"

He must not have needed to hear more detail. The wall had broken down. Although there was more to our conversation, all I remember him saying was, "Tim knew you loved him." That had never been a doubt in my mind but it was a sense of relief that Tim knew he was loved and he also knew that I could not condone his lifestyle.

That evening at the visitation as I stood beside Tim's lifeless body in the casket, Alvin came to stand beside me. He put his arm around me and the two of us shared some thoughts about Tim. The next day at the funeral those closest to Tim walked into the church for the service two by two—Mom and Dad, Jim and Sheryl, Jan and Dave, Mary Ann and Gil, and then there was me (Terry had not made the flight from Arizona to Wisconsin). And there was Alvin—alone also. So he and I walked in together in that two-by-two formation toward the front rows and sat together for the funeral and it was good. Sin never results in good but God gives grace, forgiveness, and restoration to all who are willing to receive it, whether to the one who feels like the offended or the one who feels like the offender.

Jim helped Alvin take some baby steps as a believer in Jesus during the time they had spent caring for Tim and now during his stay at Jim and Sheryl's home. Jim stood up again as he had done at the first funeral service and this time, to the family and friends he shared among other things, "I lost my brother…and I gained a brother in Christ."

It was all very clear that God was working in ways we never would have imagined. God had arranged that trip before Tim had any idea that his health was declining. Mom, Dad, Jim, and Sheryl were just the ones who needed to be with him during his last days.

Dad and Mom had done their job parenting, knowing they had not been perfect parents. In spite of the mistakes they had made, they were faithful in loving and praying for their son. God heard the cry of their hearts and answered, and Tim had come home.

CHAPTER 18

A Win-Win Situation

"Girls, look at your dad's stomach and see what you think it is."
Never one to seek out attention Dad hesitated. If concerned, he didn't
show it. Mom insisted and proceeded to raise Dad's shirt. Neither Janice
the RN, nor I, the LPN, could identify the blotches of red scattered over
his abdomen. Dad saw several doctors who had differing opinions and
treatments for the next few months. Topical prescriptions had not
worked. Radiation had not been effective. The blotches gradually
continued to spread.

"It's not painful. I feel fine," Dad said. Finally the doctors agreed
with the family that maybe someone at Mayo in Rochester could
diagnose the blotchy rash. They seemed relieved to pass this mysterious
case on to someone else.

Though the Mayo doctor demonstrated a sensitive and caring spirit,
his diagnosis was clear and he was direct with his words. "It's cancer
tunneling beneath the skin, Mr. McDowell. You have three choices. Do
nothing and you maybe have four months. Do a mild form of treatment
and you will get a few extra months. Do an aggressive chemo treatment

and you might live eight or nine months. You talk it over with your family and we can set in motion the option you choose. Facilities in La Crosse are equipped to deliver whatever treatment you decide upon."

Mom and Dad, Jim and Sheryl, and Janice, the RN daughter, went to lunch in Rochester in disbelief. Mary Ann and I were on a conference call with them from Minneapolis and Phoenix so the whole family heard the pros and cons of each option the doctor had presented. Dad made the decision to go for the mild treatment. Janice was already there for one of her quarterly trips to La Crosse and treatments at Mayo in Rochester for severe headaches and neck pain. She and Dave would extend their time in La Crosse so they could help out during Dad's first treatment which was scheduled for the end of October.

Dad came home from that first outpatient treatment so weak that Janice, even with her own health issues, had to basically carry him in from the van. At that time he weighed almost 200 pounds. He was so sick, Janice and Mom questioned if he would even live through the night. When he did survive, it was still questionable if he would ever regain his strength. Right then it was obvious his body would not be able to tolerate even this mild treatment.

Janice and Dave extended their visit and started putting into motion the plan for hospice to step in. I flew into Minneapolis where Dave and Jan were waiting with the van to drive me to La Crosse. During the drive from Minneapolis to La Crosse, Jan gave me a report just as nurses do when one shift passes off responsibilities to the next. She shared the current system of comfort measures, the potential problems, and other such things that two nurse daughters would consider in giving the best of care to their dad.

Dad and Mom were searching for an extra blanket for me, their Arizona daughter, when the three of us walked in. Dad so wanted to

154

ease his daughters' concern that he did a little jig. Janice and I panicked, thinking that he had stumbled. Chuckling, he assured us he had been in total control. He just wanted his two anxious girls to know—or at least to think—he was okay.

Dad had recovered from the reaction to the initial treatment and really did seem okay until it came time to remove his shirt. Janice and I smothered warm lotion on his abdomen and now on his back where more tumors were growing beneath the surface of his skin. It required two people to get him ready for bed. Either Jim or Aunt Ona came each evening to help me after Janice and Dave returned to Florida. At least one of us four kids was with Mom and Dad every day from this time on through Dad's illness. I had the most flexible schedule so I was there the majority of the next four months. Each evening ended with a game right after supper and then the nightly bedtime routine would start.

Hospice caregivers came twice a week and took over the morning personal hygiene care responsibilities. Janice and I gave the best nursing care we could for our dad, but we knew we had skilled help and advice available as well. Hospice let us know they did not expect us to be Dad's nurses. We were to focus on being his daughters. That took some pressure off us because we did not have all the answers. They explained what to anticipate and offered helpful hints for solving challenges as new issues surfaced.

Morning patterns were more consistent with what had been normal for Dad and Mom. Breakfast had been followed by Bible reading and prayer. In addition to that routine, Dad would prepare a blessing for his family, often based on the devotions of the morning. Usually his blessing was something related to spiritual growth, encouragement, or tidbits of wisdom he wanted to pass on to the family. (Toward his last days he did need help to put what he was doing or concerned about into words as a blessing.)

Grandchildren and other relatives wanted to keep abreast of how Dad was doing so Jim brought a laptop over to the house and set up internet connection. Generally whichever one of us was with Mom and Dad for the day would send out email updates each evening. The updates were not completed until Dad's blessing was added. These were like his last words to his loved ones that came to have special meaning for the family. The daily update expanded beyond the family. Requests came in from many others asking to be included on the "send to" list.

Mary Ann so wanted to participate in Dad's care, but Gil's needs pretty much kept her confined to Minneapolis. His stroke years earlier had left him physically handicapped. In recent months his challenges increased as well as his need for more daily care from Mary Ann. Even though she could not be in La Crosse, she managed the ever-growing list of people requesting the daily emails. Sometimes she took over writing the updates after our phone conversations regarding the news of the day and she would add the blessing prepared for the day.

Each of us kids participated in Dad's care according to the abilities and availability each of us had been gifted with. Jim managed all the room rearrangements for medical equipment that came into the house, as well as helping apply lotion to Dad's chest and back. He also created a call bell for Dad, using a doorbell mounted on a three-by-five-inch portable board. With one little press on the button, the chimes could be heard wherever any of us were in the house. He also, as is so typical of Jim, provided humor in casual conversation.

Dad believed that as long as God gave him days to live, He also had work for him to do. Much of that work at this time in his life involved encouraging and praying for people. Mom and Dad had a history of people sharing personal challenges and concerns with them. People knew confidences they shared would be kept private and that Mom and Dad really would pray for them. After so many years they ceased to be shocked about what people might share. Big or small requests, it didn't matter; God cares about whatever is troubling us.

Dad and Mom were greatly loved by all age groups. Every day people stopped in. One day the daily update recorded sixteen people had come to visit. Sometimes one car would leave just in time for the next car to pull into the vacated parking spot. Sometimes people brought in meals, sometimes desserts, and I would put on the coffeepot for fellowship around the table.

One couple stopped on their way home from the hospital with their newborn baby. Another day Jim wheeled Dad outside to enjoy the first hints of spring. A friend was driving by and saw them so she stopped. She had just lost her father and her sorrow was fresh. Mom and I had been out shopping, but when we came home Dad said he had invited this friend to join us for supper. No problem, there was always room for one more at the table.

Children came, likely prepped by parents to be extra good because Mr. McDowell was sick. Sometimes the children knew he was dying. Where he used to tease them, or connect with them in so many creative ways which made kids feel special or loved, he was now limited physically. Still he would reach out with his cane in a teasing way. Dad would find a way to interact with the children and they would know he was still the same man they had known and loved.

It's hard to tell who is enjoying this interaction the most. Dad could always find a fun way to let kids know he cared for them.

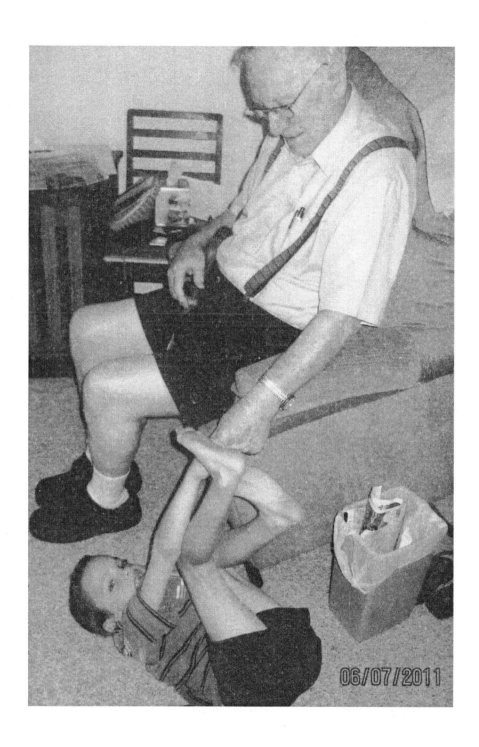

159

One day a family came with their kids who, this time, were uncharacteristically standoffish. The children stood with hands behind their back and their eyes wide open looking at Dad in the wheelchair. Dad looked at them with the proverbial tease in his eyes and asked, "I wonder if you could help me with something?"

Of course they would. They would do anything they could for this grandpa. To be able to help him would be an honor. They would set aside their hesitation and come closer to him.

"I have this problem," he said. "I have so much candy and I was wondering if you could help me with it." He extended the candy dish and the ice was broken. They chewed on their candy and chatted with him as they had done in the past.

One lady came to visit and pray for Dad. She came with concern for him but after briefly answering her question about how he was doing, he moved on to, "Now tell me how are things going with your husband's new business." As had been his habit, Dad set aside his own challenges to focus on others. Though his time here was limited, he would still reach out to others to address their needs.

Another time a friend brought a teen and his single mom who together had been full-time caregivers for the grandma in their lives. This grandma had just passed away. Mom and Dad listened as the mother shared her grief. The teen had little to say while his mother poured out her heart. After Mom and Dad prayed for them, Dad turned to the teen and started a conversation. He was good at drawing out people who did not usually converse freely. Soon they were discussing the upcoming summer Bible camp. "Camp would be a great place to make friends," he told the teen. As the conversation continued, Dad added, "Jim will be leading a group from Arrowhead Camp to the Rocky Mountains this summer. He can talk to you about going and help get you registered."

(Jim did, and this teen did go.)

Dad had been involved with the Arrowhead Bible Camp since its beginnings and saw firsthand the value of camp in the lives of kids. He, Jim, and many others had been participating together from the time the camp was only a vision. They had been a part of the hands-on hard work as God developed this camp into what it had become. In a much prayed-for but a seemingly impossible way, God arranged for Dad's oldest grandson to get from Arizona to the Rockies to join Jim and this group of teen campers.

One day a call came from the hospice director with a request. "The local newspaper asked us about doing a story regarding how those in hospice deal with Christmas when they know it will probably be their last one. Would your dad be willing to have them interview him and have his story included in their article for the La Crosse Tribune?"

Yes, he would do that and the date for the interview was set. A writer for the paper arrived with her notebook and list of questions, along with the photographer. The hospice chaplain and director also came. The photographer flashed more photo shots than what would ever be needed. The interviewer asked questions and got answers she wasn't expecting. So, she asked basically the same thing but from other approaches and still she got the same answers. She was not going to get a sad gloom-and-doom story from Dad. He said, "No matter what happens, I am in a win-win situation. If I die soon I will be with the Lord in heaven and if I live longer I will have more time with my wife and family. I can't lose."

"But this is probably your last Christmas. Are you going to do anything different for this year?"

"No, nothing will be different. As many of the family [meaning his and Mom's family, plus his siblings and their families] as can make the

161

trip will be at my sister's house for the day. We always go to Elsie's place for holidays now. Just being together is the best part of celebrating Christmas."

With her notes finished and as she prepared to leave, Mom asked her, "When will this be in the paper?"

She didn't know. "The editor determines when it will be published and where it will be located in the paper. I would suspect it will be in the Community section but I don't know when."

On Saturday, December 17, 2011, the paper's front page headline story read "Nearing the End" with two pictures of Dad beneath the headline. The article read that Dad's approach to celebrating his last Christmas was not consistent with others the writer had interviewed for this story. It either was a slow day for news or the editor must have thought that this was a newsworthy story since he chose to place it on the front page.

Though many visitors stopped in during weekdays, the highlight of each week continued to be attending church on Sunday mornings.

There would always be someone at church watching for Dad and Mom's red van. Every Sunday someone would have a wheelchair ready and help transfer Dad into it. Consistently there would be a lineup of people coming to greet them. On the Sunday of Dad's ninety-fifth birthday he had a fan club surrounding him in the foyer shortly after arriving at church. Young and old gathered around him spontaneously singing "Happy Birthday." This church had grown since the early days of the fifties and now averaged an attendance of close to two thousand. Few church members were so honored as to have their birthday acknowledged in such a way.

One who was so quick to take over maneuvering Dad's wheelchair through the crowd was a high school senior who chose to be there to help Dad rather than to be with his peers in the youth group. Dad had attended this fellow's sporting events whenever he could from the time this fellow was in elementary school. Now he was his high school's football, basketball, and track star. Dad had encouraged him all those years and now this teen was there for Dad.

The children's pastor from the church also stopped in to check on Dad. So typical of Dad, he turned the conversation away from himself to inquire about the children's ministries. Before the pastor left, he wanted to pray for Dad. As soon as he finished praying, Dad started praying for him and his ministry. Dad was pretty weak by this time, yet he was concerned about carrying on the message of Jesus to the next generation.

Another day when some Christian friends who had come from quite a distance to visit were going to leave, Dad said,

"We don't have to say 'good-bye,' we'll just say, 'so long, I'll see you later.'" Dad knew that life in heaven was ahead for him, not because of anything he had done other than believe that God's Word is true and God is faithful to His Word.

The message never gets too old, or too hard, or too outdated, or even changes. Since the time Dad had embraced this message at twenty-seven years of age, he had grown in his relationship with the Lord Jesus, and his life showed it. Because of God's Word he had peace about his future. "For God so loved the world that he gave his only begotten Son, that whosoever believeth in him should not perish, but have *everlasting* life" (John 3:16, emphasis added). Dad knew his life would continue beyond death. "I am the way, and the truth, and the life: no man cometh unto the Father but by me" (John 14:6). Jesus said there is no other way.

Eternity is too long to be wrong about this. It's a matter of "Do I believe the Bible or do I trust in what *I* think?" Another thing to consider is the question, "Have *I ever* been wrong about anything before? Should I base my eternity on what *I* think or upon what God has revealed in His Word?" Why wonder about something as important as knowing where a person will spend his forever, when God makes it so clear that a person can know for sure. Why not make that decision to receive that gift He offers? A gift does not belong to a person until he receives it. All these things are exactly what Dad would say.

Thanks to Jim, Valentine's Day 2012 was a very special day for the sweethearts of close to seven decades. Jim presented Dad and Mom with an invitation for that evening. The instructions were that semiformal attire for the event was required.

On February fourteenth Jim arrived early and helped Dad dress in a white shirt and nice pants while Mom primped herself for their last Valentine's date together. Jim fussed awhile in the kitchen and then made a quick trip to the basement. Sheryl arrived to celebrate this Valentine's mystery date with her husband and his parents.

When Jim resurfaced, he was dressed in a tux with a white folded towel over his arm. He announced to his parents and his wife, "Your table is ready." There was only one table in the house at which they ate their meals every day. But for this day Jim had set the table formally, highlighted by a centerpiece of roses and candles.

Jim extended his arm and escorted his mother and then his wife to the table. He pushed Dad to the table and secured the wheelchair locks. Then Jim reverted back to his role as maitre d`. "Later this evening we will have live entertainment in honor of sweethearts on this Valentine's day. For your dining pleasure tonight may I suggest one of three menu choices." He proceeded to offer three different meals. Actually no matter what they chose they would get chicken, potatoes, and green beans; however, each item had different descriptive titles. He presented the first choice with a detailed tantalizing fancy-sounding description of each featured item. The next choice had a French flair-sounding presentation, and the third choice was presented as southern down-home-country-style grub. He served Mom and Dad and Sheryl the salads, then, he presented the main course according to the verbal description each had chosen. The dinner was complete with a fudge brownie topped with creamy ice cream drizzled with dark chocolate syrup.

Later Jim assisted Dad in transferring from the wheelchair to the sofa and helped him extend his arm around Mom who was seated close enough to be cuddled. The music pastor and his wife, special friends of the family, arrived. Melodies and words of love songs flooded the room and filled the hearts. A few tears watered the eyes of those who were savoring this special day. It was an evening where love of friends, of family, and of husbands and wives merged. Cupids on cards may not have been present, but clearly the love that springs from the heart of God was there.

Right in the middle of all this wonderfulness Dad got a nosebleed. Though this was not a problem that accompanied his illness, still it was a reminder that life was slipping away.

Jim serving love with humor and elegance on Valentine's Day

Valentine's Day with six weeks left to live and love.

CHAPTER 19

Last Days

God knows all things and even appoints the number of our days. "Your eyes saw my unformed body; all the days ordained for me were written in your book before one of them came to be" (Psalm 139:16 NIV). Of course we didn't know how long Dad had left. But we did know the time was inevitably drawing to a close for him to be with us here on earth.

Three weeks earlier it seemed that Dad's work was done. Shortly after getting him transferred to the bath chair, his head went back and his eyes glossed over. I called, "Mom, if you want to tell Dad anything else, this is the time." His muscles totally relaxed and he seemed to be unconscious. The hospice nurse arrived. While searching for his weak pulse she shook her head, seeming to confirm my suspicion, but Dad recovered!

By early evening when Jim, his kids, and some of Jim's grandchildren came to say their good-byes (they had been called earlier in the day about Dad's crisis), Dad was alert and visiting with them. They reminisced about earlier times of camping experiences. Dad told his great-grandchildren about the time he almost got a traffic ticket and about the time he did get one. He told a granddaughter how she reminded him so much of Mae when they were young. It was an evening of saying good-bye with laughter and tears.

I kept my bedroom door open at night, wanting to make sure I could hear Dad if he needed me. Though the call bell Jim had made for him was at his side when we settled him in bed for the night, it would often get lost under his covers so it was not a dependable system at this point. It didn't take much of a stir in the living room to wake me. Sometimes I would get up and sit at the dining room table where I could observe him without him being aware of my presence. Often he would be praying. One time I grabbed a pen to write down his words. It was like a holy hush, hearing Dad speaking so personally with the Lord.

Dad's words that I heard that night and recorded were: "So many things on my mind." "Looking forward to spending more time with You." "So thankful…Your blessings…our children…the church." "Peace and comfort for our hearts and minds." "You will be there for them…they will be faithful." "The quicker we can get to Your house…." "You are a prayer-answering God." "Encourage each one." "You have our best interests at heart." "…Group of people…" "Thank You for Your faithfulness over these many, many years." "Any place where people gather, give them strength to carry on…" "Times in the past…." "Bless…." And then in a louder voice Dad cried out, "Come and help pray." Between these phrases Dad was speaking more but his words were too soft for me to hear.

Another night I was watching over him from the dimly lit dining room. He had been praying again, but I could not catch many of his words. About six in the morning there was a clunking and banging outside. The garbage truck was picking up the trash barrel and dumping

170

it along with the neighbor's trash. Right after that, the recycling truck came along. Again there was the clunking and banging sound of that truck picking up the recycling container. It just seemed so inappropriate to invade such a holy moment with such earthly things as the trash. Yet it was such a picture of life.

Dad at that very moment was focused on the Lord and spending eternity with Him shortly. Everything of this world would soon be left behind. His earthly personal possessions would be thrown out or recycled to others. It was a moment to ponder what in life is worth living for—that which will last forever or that which is only temporary? A plaque hangs on a wall in their home that reads, "Only one life will soon be past, only what's done for Christ will last." That was not just a plaque, but a motto that characterized Mom and Dad's lives.

~

A phone call interrupted the rhythmic hum of the oxygen concentrator. Dad had been so pale and weak. The cancer by now at the end of March had firmly gripped his body. Listening for Mom to answer, I stayed at my post watching over Dad for any signs that would warrant intervention—not for healing, but for comfort. From Dad's bedside I could hear Mom's side of the phone conversation. "He's so weak today...I don't know." Another short pause... "Well, just for a little while."

Today would be like so many others had been: visitors would be stopping in. So many wanted to come to visit Dad or pray with him just one more time.

Thus it was, on Sunday afternoon of March 25, 2012. The friends who had called earlier arrived. True to their promise, they stayed briefly…long enough for a short prayer and their final good-byes. He was ready to sleep after they left.

Sheryl and I took those quiet moments to go out for fresh air and a walk while Jim and Mom stayed with Dad. When we returned the scene had changed. Dad was awake and agitated. He was crying and praying for his family, letting the family who was around him know how much he loved each one. Then with such earnestness he pled, "Lord, take me home now." And again, "Lord, take me home now." He was so ready. He quieted and waited, fully expecting to enter into the presence of the Lord. After a while he calmly said, "Nothing happened. I guess my work is not finished yet." He paused and then continued, "Not my will but Thine be done."

The hospice nurse came. She asked him if he had heard anyone call his name. "No," he answered.

She said, "If you do, don't hesitate to go." His vitals were surprisingly strong and he appeared to be stable. He was relaxed now and went to sleep. It was evening when he awoke and was willing to take a few bites of lemon pie. The diabetic restrictions were a thing of the past by now.

It was time to call for Mary Ann and Janice to come. Mary Ann would drive from Minneapolis the next morning. She anticipated this time coming and had arrangements in place for Gil's needs for a day or, if necessary, two days. Janice called back saying the soonest they could book a flight from Florida would get them into La Crosse Tuesday evening.

Mom, Jim, and I hunkered down for the night to get some rest while we could. Jim would stay for the night and sleep on the sofa next to Dad's hospital bed. He woke up when Dad got restless and glanced at the clock. It was 10:45. Again Dad was asking the Lord to take him home and again as he had done so many times, he prayed for his family, his church family, and his Arrowhead Bible Camp family. Mom and I woke up too. Jim pulled a recliner up to Dad's bedside and Mom reclined there beside him, holding Dad's hand. There were short times of Dad being quiet but mostly he was talking. He repeated hundreds of times it seemed, and as fast as he could, "I love you, Mae" and "Goodnight, Mae" and "Good-bye, Mae."

Often Mom would smile and say, "Yes, I know. Can you rest now?" Those of us around his bed would sing hymns that we knew Dad liked. One that he especially wanted to hear was "All for Jesus."

"Are you in pain, Dad?"

"No, but my heart hurts." He was not talking about physical pain.

At another time he began saying names of his siblings—Alberta, Blaine, Maurice, Jenny, and Jessie, and Etta, Elsie, Beulah, Alida, Hugh, and Ruth and Ruby. He did not list them in the order of their birth. He just named each one of them apparently as he thought of each one without missing anyone. Then he began praying for all eleven of his grandchildren mentioning each one and their mates. Mom asked him about his great-grandchildren and he began praying for the oldest and went down the list naming each one in the order they were born into their families. Mom helped coach him, but he was fully aware. When they were listing Mary Ann's grandsons, Mom said the youngest one first and Dad corrected her with the name of the firstborn. He knew the right order even if Mom didn't at that moment. Then Dad said, "We have thirty-two great-grandchildren."

Mom corrected him. "Fritz, we have thirty. Scott and his wife just had their baby two weeks ago." Matt and Becky would have their third baby in about four months so it would have been understandable for Dad to say thirty-one but no, Dad was pretty adamant. "We have thirty-two." Later one grandchild, Joy, admitted that they had just found out that they were expecting. Joy shared that it was a special blessing to think that Grandpa had prayed for this new baby who was at the time known only to her and her husband.

At one point Dad appeared to be looking up with a smile. "Do you see heaven?" Jim asked.

"Ya."

Jim asked what it looked like but Dad gave no answer.

At another time during the night Dad got a big smile on his face and said, "I'm Fritz McDowell from La Crosse, Wisconsin, and my license is..." and he named off numbers that were not familiar...maybe his car license. He continued, "And my Dad's license is...oh, I can't remember right now," and he got agitated with himself for forgetting.

I said, "Don't worry about that. Jim will take care of it," and Dad settled down.

Dad had been talking pretty much nonstop through much of the night while Jim was resting on the sofa. "Shh," I said. "We have to be quiet, Jim is trying to sleep." Dad lifted his head to look over at Jim and responded "Oh, oh, oh, I'll be quiet." And he was for a very short time. Knowing that someone would need to be awake the next day, Jim ended up going to the basement to get a little sleep.

Later Dad went on as if he was introducing someone to his family. "This is my wife, Mae. We are Fritz and Mae from La Crosse. And I want to introduce you to my daughter Stella. And I want to introduce you to my daughter Mary Ann. And I want to introduce you to my daughter Janice. And my son Jim. My son Jim, he's a good man."

Mom whispered, "Don't forget Tim," and Dad added, "Oh, yes, Tim." It seemed like Dad was introducing his family to someone from heaven! Since Tim was already there, wouldn't it be understandable that

174

he would consider it not necessary to introduce him?

After such a busy night, Dad slept all day Monday. Some of the McDowell family came and were sitting in the living room around his bed conversing with Mom. Dad seemed to be sleeping throughout their visit—and on through the whole night.

Janice called right before she and Dave boarded their plane Tuesday morning. Mom put the phone to Dad's ear. Though he had not spoken since during the early hours of Monday morning, when he heard Janice's voice he said a weak "Hi." Janice told him that just hearing his voice was a precious gift. They would arrive in La Crosse at 8:30 p.m.

Dad was sleeping when the hospice nurse arrived to help me reposition him later that Tuesday morning. She advised, "If you want any chance of him living until Jan arrives, don't try to reposition him again."

Every breath was a blessing that meant life for one more minute at a time. As the minutes ticked away, each quarter hour was counted as a major step in reaching that 8:30 p.m. goal. Mary Ann had come earlier. By mid-afternoon we felt that God would honor Dad and the family by letting him live until Jan and Dave would arrive and we could all be together.

At 8:30 Janice rushed into the house. The last word he had said was his one word greeting to Janice that morning on the phone. Other than raising his eyebrows at times, he was not responding. But his family responded with tears and yet joy for this gift of being together again. Janice and Mary Ann were at Dad's bedside most of Tuesday night.

I woke up about 5:30 knowing that there was still one thing Dad could do. Janice especially had wanted Dad to give her a blessing like Jacob had done for his sons. Dad had never followed through, not because he was not willing. More likely he never thought he knew how to give his children the kind of blessing he thought Janice wanted. During the night the Lord brought to my mind the blessing Aaron, the priest, used to bless the children of Israel with from Numbers 6:24-26.

Dad was still the head of his family; he still had authority to pray a blessing over his family. Second Peter refers to believers as being a royal priesthood. Why not have Dad bless Janice now? As soon as I knew Mom was awake I went to her room and presented an idea. Mom agreed.

At breakfast Mom shared the plan with the rest of the family. After breakfast the four kids and Mom knelt beside Dad's bed and rested his hand on Janice's head. I recited the blessing from the book of Numbers. "May the LORD bless you and keep you. May the LORD make his face to shine upon you and be gracious unto you. May the LORD lift up His countenance upon you and give you peace" (Numbers 6:24-26 NASV). "Lord, we don't mean to put words in Dad's mouth that he would not have spoken. We are asking for You to remember Dad's prayers that he has petitioned You for in the past for Janice, and especially those prayers right now for her health. Amen."

Then we put Dad's hand on Mary Ann's head and repeated the Numbers 6 blessing. We asked for a renewal of all the prayers Dad had spoken on Mary Ann's behalf. Then we placed Dad's open hand on Jim's head. I repeated again the priestly blessing for Jim and a prayer again asking God to remember Dad's prayers for this son. Mom then said, "Jim, you do it now for Stella." So, with Dad's hand on my head, Jim spoke the words of the Numbers 6 blessing and asked God to remember the prayers Dad had prayed for me. Last, our ninety-year-old mom knelt beside the bed and put Dad's hand on her own head and again the blessing of Numbers 6 was repeated with the request for a renewal of Dad's prayers for her.

Dave was the only in-law present. From the dining room he had been watching the family circled around Dad. "Dave, you come too." Mom extended her arm to Dave. "You can represent all the mates." So, Dave, representing Terry, Gil, and Sheryl, as well as himself, was blessed and prayed for in the same way.

It was a precious time of praying and crying together. It was also a time of sighing relief. The time had come now to let go. It seemed that Dad had done all he could do. His work was finished. This must have been true because his breathing changed about 11:30 a.m. March 28, 2012.

We were all at his bedside, and Mom was holding his hand as Dad slipped from mortality to immortality...from our presence into the presence of the Lord. God had preserved his life until Dad had finished his work.

The nurse daughters lowered the head of his bed while Jim looked up and called out, "Dad, we're going to be okay." Then Jim made the call for the hospice nurse to come. For the first time Dad did not look like Dad. There was no sparkle in his eyes or even a hint of life on his face. Truly, the body is just the shell of a person. Dad's temporary body had served him well for ninety-five years. But now, he was more alive than ever, though not in our presence.

The nurse arrived and confirmed what the family already knew. Jim had called the pastor who arrived and joined us downstairs in one of the rooms Dad had remodeled when they had moved in nine years earlier. Together we started the process of making the arrangements for celebrating his life. The nurse finished what needed to be done and came downstairs saying she was leaving.

It was so quiet upstairs. The oxygen concentrator had been turned off and set aside. Dad's hospital bed had been made. That wonderful hospice nurse had found one of the Green Bay knit caps Dad had made for so many people during his last months. It sat at the head of the otherwise empty bed.

Dad was gone but proof of his life being lived was still very present. He had left a legacy and the effects of his ninety-five years here would continue to impact the lives of those who had been touched by him. For how long? Time will tell, but that is not up to him. He lived life with the goal of being faithful to the Lord. Some may boast of treasures or trinkets left to them; we are blessed with his footprints, his life story. Dad's greatest joy would be that his life would lead others to Jesus. Then, as Dad had said before, "We don't have to say good-bye. We can just say, 'see you later'."

CHAPTER 20

BLESSINGS BY EMAIL

Evening blessings came about by accident. Toward the end of Dad's life, so many phone calls came in from family wanting to know about the events of the day and how Dad was doing that we realized we couldn't take time to repeat the same info for each call every evening so we moved to nightly emails. It just seemed natural to have a word of encouragement or something special Dad wanted to convey to the family at the end of each email. Thus, the idea of a blessing to end each day seemed like a loving way to connect with the family. Soon more requests came in for those updates and blessings. To some those blessings were like last words from a physical or spiritual patriarch. Some of those blessings may be meaningful to others. Many have wonderful parents who have spoken blessings into their lives, still the words of a godly man have value for any who want to be blessed by them. We, as Dad's kids, willingly share those blessings with you who have come to know Dad through the pages of this book.

- January 29—You are blessed to be a blessing to others.

- February 4—My greatest joy is to see you walking with the Lord. That is the greatest reward a parent can have. May the Lord be your companion as you walk through life.

- February 5—May you have self-discipline to make it a priority to assemble with other believers to worship the Lord.

- February 6—May the Lord set a guard over your lips so you do not speak negative words that bring pain or wound spirits. The Lord bless you with pleasant words, profitable advice, and kind speech in all your conversations.

- February 7—Express thanks to the Lord for something specific today.

- February 8—Turn your lives over to the Lord. Pay close attention to His Word and follow Him.

- February 9—By example teach your children good work habits. But learn again with them the joy of playing together.

- February 10—Listen to your kids and grand-children; consider what they have to say. Enjoy time with them.

- February 11—May the Lord bless you with a teachable spirit, with ears to hear the heart of those God has placed in your life.

- February 14—The Lord bless you with a growing appreciation, love, and commitment to the mate God has given to you.

- February 18—Teach your children the difference between right and wrong by your example.

- February 20—God promised He will be there for you no matter what you are going through.

- February 22—We are just an ordinary family, but God can still use you in extraordinary ways to bring glory to Him.

- February 26—Pass the message of the Good News of Christ to your next generation.

- February 27— "Trust in the Lord with all thine heart and lean not unto thy own understanding. In all thy ways acknowledge him, and he shall direct thy paths" (Proverbs 3:5-6).

- February 29—Aspire to be someone known for warmth and wisdom.

- March 1—Be a wise steward of all that God has entrusted to you.

- March 3—Pray for the next generations, even those not yet born, that each one will know Jesus.

- March 4—Never miss a chance to say, "I love you."

- March 8—Be in the Word. Be encouraged. God will guide you.

- March 9—Depend on Him—not on your own strength whether physical, intellectual, or financial.

- March 11—May the Lord bless you as you use the gifts and talents He has given you for His glory.

- March 12—May you always have a reverent fear of the Lord and respect for His Word. This is the source of wisdom.

- March 14—Dad's blessing came from the Our Daily Bread today. A trapeze artist may be the star of the show but the real star is the teammate who hangs from another trapeze bar to reach out and grab him. Dying must be something like trusting God as the catcher. After we have flown through life, we can look for God to reach out to

182

catch His followers and pull us safely to Himself forever.

- March 16h—The Lord bless you with faith to step boldly into the unknown with confidence that He will be with you in your future just as He has been in the past.

- March 22—For J-O-Y, put Jesus first, others next, and yourself last.

- March 23—Jim wrote as Dad was not able tonight: I am blessed to have Dad as my example. I know as I attempt to follow in his steps I will not go wrong. Dad would be the first to say he is not perfect, but he has shown me the way to be a Christian man.

- March 24—Dad's blessing tonight is his example. Even in his weakness today when the pastor came, Dad prayed for him and the ministry of the church. He compared the church to a lighthouse that would be a place where the community would be drawn to the Light. He prayed that God would show each of us what we can do to further God's kingdom. At this age and weak as he was today, he still wants to serve the Lord.

- March 25—Be ready. No one knows the time or date of one's last moment on earth. Dad asked the Lord to take him home today but concluded that his work must not be done yet because God didn't take him yet.

- March 26—As hard as this day has been to watch Dad transition from mortality to immortality, we are not alone. Only because of Jesus we know that Dad could rest with the assurance that it was well with his soul.

- March 27—Janice arrived. We are together and with Dad. Cherish times with your family.

- March 28—at 11:45 a.m. Dad went home to be with the Lord. It was a very peaceful time; a bittersweet time. Dad said just a couple days ago that he didn't have any pain but his heart hurt. That's how we feel today.

CHAPTER 21

ALONE...YET, NOT ALONE

It seemed the end of an era had come. Contributing to the celebration of Dad's life were pictures, shared memories, and the packed church representing individuals whose lives had been impacted because Dad, along with Mom, had made time to care about each of them. Following the service, friends and family conversed over a lunch of pizza just as many had done with Mom and Dad for so many pizza get-togethers before. As the crowd thinned down, we packed up flowers, cards, and leftover pizza to take home to the empty house.

We knew we had to get back to our homes and responsibilities, but we would not leave Mom alone right away. The day the first one of us had to head to the airport, the four of us siblings and Mom wrapped our arms around each other making a circle of only five and we prayed, thanking the Lord for blessing us with Dad and asking for the Lord's comfort and help in the days ahead, knowing that we would each experience waves of sorrow.

We prayed especially for Mom and all the adjustments ahead for her. Each of us would continue to use our gifts and abilities as needed to help Mom just as we had done in caring for Dad.

Eventually Mom's first day and first night to be alone arrived and the house was quiet—quieter than it had ever been. No one was there to help her take the next step for what she needed to do. No one was there to hold her hand or give a comforting hug. No one was there to carry on a conversation with her.

When Dad had taken his last breath, Jim had called out to him, "Dad, we're going to be okay." Mom knew that would be true but sometimes, the eighteen inches between the head and the heart seemed more like a huge gulf.

The hole in her heart could not be ignored. Widow! She was not prepared for this new identity. Sixty-eight years earlier she had been prepared for her part of the Mr. and Mrs. McDowell title and the Fritz and Mae references. Especially since Dad's retirement, they had done everything together and rarely was she referred to without Dad's name attached to hers. Now she was Mae or Mom—only half of the unit of one she and Dad had become. She had never felt like a half person before.

Little things, common things taken so for granted before, triggered memories and tears, like the day she sorted through his personal belongings that were no longer needed and picked up his wallet. Through the years Mom never had to ask Dad for money. True, they were usually together and he would pay for what they bought. But he always checked her purse to make sure she had money available and if she was low on cash, he would slip in a twenty-dollar bill. He knew she was not a person to buy unnecessary items on impulse and she would be wise in her spending. He had always made sure she was provided for. She went through his billfold weeping at the sight of seeing what he had always carried with him...the pictures of them as newlyweds and us kids as young children. These were what he considered his valuables. The billfold was old and worn but she would keep it. His provision for her from what had passed through this billfold was a token of his love and care. She knew she was blessed.

How different it had been for her own mother. She had been crippled from a childhood accident and life as a poor farmer's wife had been hard. With one crutch under her arm she had taken care of the children, raised big gardens each year, hunted for lost cows, and everything else that went into such a farm life. Mom's father had been a harsh man and lashed out in anger at his crippled wife if she even brought up the need for a pair of shoes or some other necessity for one of their seven children. When one of Mom's siblings brought up memories of those childhood beatings inflicted upon them by their father, Mom confirmed what they said but she was not known to initiate such conversations.

A Christian neighbor had faithfully picked up the seven children and sometimes their crippled mother for Sunday school and church. That was Mae's introduction to the Bible and the news that Jesus loved her. At eleven years of age she accepted Jesus as her Savior at the evangelistic tent meeting the neighbor took them to. Mom's father was elderly before joining the rest of the family in trusting in Jesus as his Savior.

That childhood was a long time ago for this newly-widowed ninety-year old. Mom had grown over the years in her relationship with the Lord and in the biblical convictions that formed her values and decisions. She had prayed that she and Dad would leave this world together but God had said no to that request.

Even in her aloneness, she could not doubt the biblical foundation that God is Sovereign, He loves her, and He has a purpose for everything—even His answer of "not yet" regarding her prayer request. God still must have work for her to do, but it would be so different being alone. One day she shared with Janice, "I could sit here and just feel sorry for myself but I refuse to do that. Much as I hate to be alone, I need to get busy and serve the Lord however I can."

Mom and Dad had talked through some of those decisions regarding how life would change for her. Though he would not be there to drive, she should keep the red van. Jim would maintain it, and it would be available for Janice or me when we visited La Crosse. Dad felt that people who would come to drive Mom places could drive the van and he did not want to take advantage of the kindness of others by causing added wear and tear on their cars.

Dad and Mom had unintentionally invested for this time through their years of caring for so many other people. What they had done for others was now being done for Mom. They used to share produce from the Dresbach garden. Now a farming family was faithfully bringing vegetables and eggs to Mom. Mom had helped Ben in his strawberry patch; now others were coming to help Mom with her little garden space and the display of flowers that added a welcoming touch to her yard.

Mom and Dad had helped widows in their loneliness and now their church family was coming to help Mom. Sometimes ladies would call saying, "I just made a big batch of soup [or something else] and I'm bringing some over for you."

Mom's usual response would be, "Will you stay and have lunch with me when you come? It's so hard to eat alone." People from a new generation are following in Mom and Dad's footprints or tracks of serving and, in the process, are being examples for yet another generation.

Gradually Mom stepped back into activities she and Dad had done as a team. When the church first started a Food Pantry ministry for the needy in the community, Dad suggested having a table set up where people who came for food could also have someone to talk to and pray with if they chose to. He and Mom manned that prayer table until Dad could no longer participate. When Mom was ready to resume this ministry, ladies from the church provided transportation for her and then partnered with her at the prayer table.

Whether it was caramel corn or apple pies or whatever big kitchen project Mom planned, Dad had been at her side. Dad would slice apples while Mom rolled out pie crusts. They had often provided pies for church dinners for college students. Jim called one day, "Mom, I need some apple pies." He was in charge of a sportsman retreat at Arrowhead Bible Camp and thought homemade pies would be a big hit as prizes for the men. He brought the apples and took Dad's place at Mom's side peeling and slicing apples and together they made "Mae's Apple Pies". She soon was back to making pies for the college kid's meals.

Company for Sunday dinner was normal and that hasn't changed since Dad passed away. Typically, Mom does most of the preparation on Saturday and Jim, Sheryl or Aunt Ona who are usual guests along with others, take charge of the kitchen and serve what she had put in the oven earlier. She also initiates evening meals for people to come and then play games after the table is cleared.

The activity Mom had participated in for several years involved meeting with mostly elderly ladies every Wednesday, and after coffee and cake, they would crochet sweaters for missions. By the time the one-hundred-and-three-year-old-lady, who opened her home for this gathering, moved into a care center, Mom was alone so she invited the women to come to her home. They no longer were making sweaters so it had become more of a social time than a service ministry. Mom, as host for these five to twenty ladies, started inviting speakers to join the group to share or sometimes the ladies shared their testimonies.

One day the conversation turned to funeral plans and how that could be a meaningful time of witness to their families, but the question was raised about how would they leave messages they wanted conveyed. Mom went to the church office asking for forms the ladies could fill out to plan their own funerals. She passed out the forms the next week and the ladies worked on their ideas for the messages and songs they would want presented. Some commented that they did not even know the pastors who were new in the growing church. How could they make a choice for who would officiate?

Mom arranged for each of the pastors to have a day to visit the Wednesday group and speak so the ladies could get acquainted with each one and feel more comfortable about who they would choose to officiate for them. That turned out to be a blessing for the pastors to meet these senior ladies, many of whom prayed for them.

Mom is no stranger to the pastors. Sometimes they call upon her to befriend someone and share not only friendship but God's Word appropriate to their need and pray for them. She also is one who makes calls to visitors who request a contact from the church. The church has a ministry of welcoming new babies with a blanket or quilt made mostly by the ladies in Mom's Wednesday afternoon group. Mom is the usual person to contact these new moms and arrange for a home visit, if possible, to deliver the gift. Of course she goes with a younger lady who can drive so they serve as a team. Mom as the "senior saint" typically holds the baby and prays for the family and this new life. This is no small one or two blankets a year ministry. During the year of 2015 they blessed seventy-seven babies in this way!

Besides making baby quilts, she has made car loads of crafts like scrubbies, potholders, quilts, knitted hats and an assortment of other projects for funding mission projects and the retirement home where Mary Ann works. At the end of each day, she is able to look back over the day knowing she had made good use of her time interacting with people or making progress on some craft project.

The day Dad passed away, an elderly widowed neighbor lady knocked on the front door to extend her sympathies. I answered but could not understand her speech as she had lost her tongue to cancer. Mom came to greet her and seemed to understand her message if not her exact words. As Phyllis walked away, Mom said, "That lady needs a friend. I'm going to get to know her and be a friend to her."

Eventually Mom made contact and though their conversation sometimes stalled while Phyllis wrote down words she could not speak clearly, they became friends. Phyllis wanted to learn how to make scrubbies and yarn poodles. Mom mentioned one day as they worked on the crafts about how good the church people were to her and she asked Phyllis if her church people helped her. She hung her head, "No."

Mom invited her. "There's room for you in the van if you want to come to church with me." She came…and kept coming. Standing beside Mom she too received hugs and greetings from the church family. When Phyllis fell and went to a care center, Phyllis' daughter would come and get Mom and they would visit her mother. After Phyllis passed away, her family asked Mom to speak at her funeral. Phyllis had become a believer since going to church with Mom and Mom was given freedom to share about their friendship and about Phyllis knowing where she would be spending eternity and why. Mom was ninety-five when she spoke at this service.

Life in other ways had absolutely changed since Dad's passing. They had started every morning breakfast prayer with "Good morning, Lord

Jesus" and their time together of Bible reading and prayer followed breakfast. Morning prayer time starts out with the same greeting to the Lord but Mom has her quiet time with the Lord alone. People call her with special requests for prayer as they had done when Dad and she had prayed together. She prays alone but still with expectancy, asking later how God answered those requests.

Dad and Mom had made it their habit to pray together after they crawled into bed at night. Now Mom generally prays in her big chair since she is alone, knowing that she would otherwise fall asleep before completing the list of requests she wants to pray for. And then when she goes to bed, she listens to Christian music until sleep and music merge together.

She admits that it's easier to go to bed early than to deal with lonely evenings. By early evening she is tired anyway. Truly, as long as she has life, God has work for her to do. And that she does with diligence saying, "I can't let grass grow under my feet. There's much to do every day." Even when pain invades her space, she says she can still work on crafts or her quilts. She believes time is a gift not to be wasted. That plaque on the wall is as true for the remaining one as what it was when Mom and Dad served the Lord together. "Only one life will soon be past, only what's done for Christ will last."

On Mom's ninety-fifth birthday our immediate family gathered for our own Sunday morning service before the open house for extended family and friends. Jim retold the story of the disciples crossing the Sea of Galilee and the storm coming up, yet Jesus brought them safely to the other shore.

Jim turned to Mom and asked her to share some of the storms she had faced and how God brought her through them. Some great-grandchildren were hearing from her for the first time some of the events of God's faithfulness through the good and the difficult times. Then at Jim's request Mary Ann, Janice, Jim, and I shared in a couple sentences how we are currently serving the Lord. Following us, each of the grandchildren who were present also shared.

It all started with one neighbor bothering to go out of her way to take some poor farmer kids to Sunday school. From such a seemingly little thing like picking up these kids each week, God had changed and will continue to change the course of several generations for eternity. We might think what we have to offer the Lord is little, but we never know what God might do with whatever we offer to Him. Dad had always said, "We are just ordinary people," but God uses ordinary people.

A song by Steve Green that so characterizes both Dad and Mom contains the words "May those who come behind us find us faithful." They have been examples of being faithful to the Lord. Now it's our turn to carry on with the legacy we will leave behind.

ACKNOWLEDGEMENTS

I greatly appreciate my parents, Fritz and Mae McDowell and my siblings, Mary Ann, Janice, Jim and Tim for first living this story and then for allowing this intimate peek into our family life to be shared through these pages. Mary Ann, Janice, Jim, and Mom read through each chapter and added insights and memories that helped in giving an accurate picture of our lives. Elsie McDowell and a family history booklet, *Our McDowell Heritage* (compiled by Beverly McDowell, Ruby Shaw, and Jeanne Roberts) provided further information and confirmation of early family events. The referenced booklet was used with permission.

Often when the project seemed too challenging the LORD provided the nudges I needed to keep me on task. And, thanks to my husband for his practical help around the house, I could continue to write and press on to the finish line. Surely the Lord meant that the lessons of life and faith Mom and Dad experienced are to be recorded so they can touch the lives of others.

This book would be available only to family and close friends had it not been for the encouragement to consider a wider readership from my beta readers including George and Pam Clark and Debbie Roberts, and early editorial reader input from Judy Phillips and Wayne Schams.

I appreciate the expertise of my editor Donna Goodrich and her words of encouragement, the cover photography by Joy Peabody and Angela Byram, and the cover design by Grace Bridges. Bringing a book to the public takes team effort. I appreciate all those who had a part in preserving Dad and Mom's story.

Stella McDowell
Tempe, Arizona
April 2017